NICHOLAS OF FLÜ
SWISS HERMIT & P

For Mary
a friend for many years.

With many thanks & blessings.

Tom

October 1999

Nicholas of Flüe 1417 – 1487
Swiss Hermit & Peacemaker

Thomas Boos

The Pentland Press Ltd
Edinburgh · Cambridge · Durham · USA

© Thomas Boos 1999

First published in 1999 by
The Pentland Press Ltd.
1 Hutton Close
South Church
Bishop Auckland
Durham

British Library Cataloguing in Publication Data.
A catalogue record for this book is available
from the British Library.

ISBN 1 85821 656 7

Typeset by George Wishart & Associates, Whitley Bay.
Printed and bound by Antony Rowe Ltd., Chippenham.

For my Brothers and Sisters

Contents

Foreword

This study of a most remarkable Swiss, Nicholas of Flüe, has been taking shape for over thirty years. A deep interest in Nicholas led me to the places where he lived, and then to an ongoing, critical study of the sources for this extraordinary man's life. After contributing articles to various publications and reviewing other biographies, my first attempt at a full life was published by the Bethlehem Fathers, a missionary congregation based at Immensee in Switzerland.

Among the friends who have generously criticized my efforts was Dom Doyère, a French naval captain, who became a monk and later prior at St Paul de Wisques. An introduction from his pen would have been invaluable, but it was not to be. Dom Doyère felt that this biography would gain greatly were Joan of Arc, Nicholas's contemporary, introduced. Some of the many points of resemblance are mentioned in the text. Joan's place in world history as a nation-builder is well known; Nicholas's similar role merits to be highlighted.

Dom Doyère is included in my dedication, as are the many friends, who have contributed in one way or another to this book. To Agnes Dorman I am indebted for the loan of 'Jeanne d'Arc', which contained the indispensable original documents concerning the Maid of Orleans. Angela Farmer has coped bravely, deciphering my amendments for their insertion into the 'first draft'. Finally, I owe great gratitude to my wife, Anne, who encouraged me to complete what has been a labour of hope as well as of love.

Midhurst, 24 August 1998

CHAPTER I

A Son of Obwalden

In 1417 – traditionally on 21 March – Hemma von Flüe presented her husband Heinrich with their first child, a son and heir. Because there was no priest in the parish of Sachseln to which they belonged, the boy was carried, by way of the Ranft, to the church at Kerns for his baptism. He was christened Nicholas, after his maternal grandfather. The family had been remarkable, Wölflin wrote, for over 400 years, more by its integrity than by its riches. Unfortunately it is impossible to know whether this is exact. Wölflin may have confused two families with similar names: a family in Kerns, Unter der Flüe, was quite well known locally, but it is not possible to trace Nicholas's paternal ancestors. The name seems to have been derived from the title of the lands, zu Flü, where they lived. Hemma (née Rubert) was from Wolfenschiessen, a village on the Engelberger Aa in Nidwalden.

Wölflin, the first official biographer of Nicholas, wrote at the request of the Obwalden authorities and dedicated his work to Bishop (later Cardinal) Schinner in 1501, though it seems certain that he had completed it already some time before, and had received his commission to write considerably before that date. In compiling it, he had personally questioned people who had known the saint, and had had access to the parish register of Sachseln; his list of miracles does not mention any recorded after 1493, which would seem to suggest the date at which he collected his memoirs (and the description of numerous cures ascribed to Nicholas), is usually considered to have been put into writing in view of the process of canonization, an event those who knew him felt sure would one day take place. Although these memoirs are not in fact drawn up in correct legal form, this may well be the case as the Swiss were well known for their disregard of the niceties of procedure.

Background

These names plunge us into one of the forest districts (the nucleus from which Switzerland as we know it today developed), at a time when the Confederation was taking definitive shape. The original three forest districts (or cantons as they were later called), Uri, Schwyz and Unterwalden (this last made up of Obwalden and Nidwalden), have changed but little since Nicholas lived and a vivid modern description serves quite adequately as a picture of fifteenth-century Obwalden.

> Although Ur-Schweiz [John Russell kept this expression in the original language lest the translation 'primitive Switerland' deceive] includes, or is overlooked by, a great many high mountains, it is mostly made up of undulant agricultural country – orchard and pasture, with everywhere the sound of hurrying water. The fountains are never dry in the squares of Ur-Schweiz; often bowered in geraniums, they whisper quietly throughout the year, as they have whispered, in many cases, for five centuries. It rains a great deal in this country, until each roof becomes a chute of water and the countryside explores, ever more patiently, the possibilities of green. One must watch the lakes of Ur-Schweiz as they shudder and decompose beneath heavy rain; and afterwards one must pace the leafy quays and listen to the last drops of rain as they probe the foliage of chestnut and plane. One

must know this country in July, when the sun strikes down on the terrace and sucks the colour from its awnings; when the midnight sky still shimmers with the heat of the afternoon, and the wooden roofs painfully stretch and contract from hour to blazing hour. And one must come also in February, when snow gives place to grass (the colour of tobacco), and the Muota, the Seewen and the Sarneraa become torrents, milk-white and creamy, unimaginably rapid in their shallow beds. And at any season there are the huge white village churches of Ur-Schweiz . . . the typical landscape of these cantons will have in its foreground a church, surmounted by its black or gold onion and standing perhaps a little above its village, in a plantation of saturated green.

Obwalden borders on the lake of Lucerne, but after the magnificent grandeur of that lake its scenery is quiet and unassertive. It consists of a principal valley, in two storeys climbing southwards, and a secondary side valley. Sarnen, with its lake, forms the first floor of the principal valley, Lungern, and its smaller lake, the second. Branches so laden with fruit that they need a crutch to prevent them from snapping are typical in this fertile, tranquil valley. The smaller lateral valley, the Melchtal, is of quite a different nature; the Melchaa, a tumultuous stream after a storm or when the snows are melting, forces its way between rocks and pastureland until, suddenly, before it reaches the valley and the lake of Sarnen, it seems to be swallowed up in a deep narrow gorge. The wooden bridge which crosses it here is said to be the highest in Europe.

The character of the people of Obwalden has much in common with its countryside. In this still comparatively inaccessible country it is possible to make a generalization and to describe them as of a good physique, quick-witted, with a tendency to be critical, endowed with a sense of humour, alive to the beauty of the surrounding nature, enamoured of freedom and independence, and devout. Under a good-natured exterior is hidden a strength of soul, both thoughtful and tenacious; under an exterior reserve a passionateness; under a certain easy-going attitude a remarkable promptness in action. These deep-seated forces rarely appear in everyday life, but should a political discussion arise or a matter in which vital religious or local interests are at stake then 'the Melchaa roars in its depths.' But when the storm is passed the usual serenity returns. Heinrich Federer, who knew the Obwalden folk well, thought their most prominent character traits were 'a shrewdness bordering almost on slyness, and a remarkable self-discipline'.

Fundamentally the men of Obwalden have hardly changed since Nicholas of Flüe, but conditions of life are of course somewhat easier. Board and lodging as well as dress were simpler then; the farmhouses were roughly built, rooms were low, with floor and ceiling made of roughly hewn beams. Lighting was poor, furniture simple. These peasants spun their own flax and wove the material which was to clothe the whole family. Their staple diet consisted of milk, cheese and butter, bread and fruit, either fresh or dried; there was meat as well, for each autumn the farmer slaughtered one or more of his cattle, a pig, or two or three of his sheep or goats, and these provisions were then smoked and dried. Besides this meat, there was whatever had been caught hunting or fishing; game and fish abounded in the forests and lakes of Obwalden then – so abundant was the fish that there is a stipulation in the terms of employment that servants were not to be given fish at table more than three times a week! On the whole each farm produced what it needed, and the farmer was independent.

Its natural frontiers and the poor state of the roads made the district far more isolated than it is today. Bad weather made the lake route to Lucerne dangerous and even impassable, while the land route was no more than a footpath along the Lopperberg, a promontory of Mt. Pilatus, overhanging the lake. The bridle path across the Brünig into the Bernese Oberland would today be considered as impracticable, and the passages into the Entlebuch were no better. Obwalden was thus inaccessible to carriages all the year round, while in winter it was not even possible to cross the passes with mules. Few strangers came into the district and traffic was negligible, so that the people had to learn to suffice for themselves, and consequently developed an interior life.

Yet it is important to note that commerce with the exterior was much greater than this isolation would suggest. The Obwaldeners brought their cheese and butter to market to Lucerne; they crossed into the Oberland with their livestock as well. And what is after all even more noteworthy, from earliest times they frequented the markets of Northern Italy, and brought home wine, metals, hardware and finer materials. Such commerce demanded a strong physique. A group would leave each Tuesday, at one in the morning, for Alpnach, bearing their loads of about 100lb of butter; at Alpnach they would wait for the pinnace which was to carry them across the lake to Lucerne. Were the lake too rough for the pinnace to cross, they shouldered their loads once more, and climbed the slopes of the Lopperberg, then over the Reugg by the path into the town. The Italian enterprise meant crossing the Brünig, with twenty to thirty heavily laden mules, or with livestock; then, by way of the higher and wilder Grimsel Pass, the caravan wound its way into the Upper Valais, whence it descended by the often vertiginous Gries Pass into the Ticino, and on into Lombardy.

Unterwalden (that is Obwalden and Nidwalden together) with Uri and Schwyz formed in 1291 the League of the Three Forest Districts – the foundation of the Swiss Confederation. By the successive adherence of Lucerne, Bern, Zurich, Zug and Glarus, the League or Alliance of the Eight Cantons was formed. Obwalden along with the other districts sent its contingent of soldiers to the battles the Confederates fought for their political independence. Then, as now, it was an independent district, with the citizens meeting together in the open air at Sarnen to discuss local affairs, to pass or reject laws, and to elect councillors and judges. All male citizens of good repute assisted at the diet from the age of fifteen. The *Landamman*, roughly equivalent to a local governor, elected at this assembly, promised on oath to respect and defend the rights of the people, while they for their part swore obedience and loyalty to the government they had elected. Like the vast majority of the people, even leading councillors and judges were often unable to read or write, but the Obwaldeners had reached quite a high degree of civilization. The constant relations with the markets of the Lombard cities had brought them into touch with the political and religious movements, gaining ground in Italy during the twelfth, thirteenth and fourteenth centuries. These markets were not only centres of business but also centres of culture, with splendid opportunities of getting to know what was happening in Church and State, of exchanging ideas and forming opinions. To this influence from the south, we must of course add that of the towns belonging to the League: Lucerne, Bern, and Zurich.

This then is the landscape and the historical framework against which Nicholas of Flüe is to be seen adequately to appreciate his greatness.

The Family

There is certain record of only one other child born to Heinrich and Hemma von Flüe, a son, Peter, but probably there were at least two other children: a boy, Egloff, and a girl, Katherina, later the wife of Erni Rorer, a great friend of Nicholas. The family, Wölflin says, was accustomed to do good to all and sundry, and, he adds they were far more given to prayer and to assistance at church services than others, which for him was a sign of what would one day happen in the family. Like Joan of Arc's family they were fairly well-to-do farmers; pastureland and forests had seemingly been handed down from father to son; even property further away in the Melchtal belonged to them. Farming in this hilly countryside was exacting, and work in the forests like felling trees and bringing them down to the valley could be enlivened – or endangered – by bears, still wild in the fifteenth century.

Nicholas, or the shortened form Klaus, was a fairly common name in Obwalden at this time. The popularity can in part be traced to the devotion to St Nicholas of Myra, expressed and encouraged by the chapel of St Nicholas that is still standing opposite Flüeli. Hemma will often have crossed the Melchaa to visit this little church with her children. There was Mass there each week on Tuesday and Wednesday, and the von Flües certainly went there as it was nearer than their parish church, which in any case had no incumbent at this time. Klaus saw on the walls pictures depicting in detail the whole of the life of Our Lord, from the moment of the Annunciation to the Ascension; there too, for the first time, he saw pictures of St Mary Magdalen, who was to become his favourite saint. The legend of Nicholas, the holy bishop of Myra – not doubted by anyone in the fifteenth century – was illustrated in the chapel and Hemma probably talked about it to her children, and from her Klaus heard about his patron's precocious fasting on Wednesdays and Fridays at his mother's breast. At Bern and Zurich there were houses of Augustinian friars and hermits, who propagated devotion to their confrere, Nicholas of Tolentino, who though not canonized until 1446 had been popularly acclaimed a saint after his death in 1305. Thus Nicholas began at the age of seven to do unusual penances, and would go to a little cave near the town (Sant Angelo near Fermo in the March of Ancona) and pray there like the hermits, who lived at that time among the Apennines. Nicholas of Flüe surely knew of these two patrons of his, just as he knew of Matthias Hattinger, a hermit who lived in the woods near Wolfenschiessen, his mother's native village.

Praying all by himself when it was possible, doing penance of a quite unexpected nature for such a young boy, watching out to seize opportunities of getting his companions to do good – these are the traits that stand out in the descriptions of him given by Erni Rorer, a near neighbour but about nine years older than Klaus. These traits suggest the influence of the examples his mother set before him. The evidence of Rorer and An der Halden, both men of some standing, can be accepted without hesitation. Rorer's personal reminiscences are lifelike and convincing. He says that when the children came back from working in the fields or elsewhere, Klaus would give them the slip in order to pray behind a shed or in some solitary spot, letting Erni and others go off to play. These children, who were expected to lend a hand as best their age and size allowed, were probably a lively set of youngsters and the detail that Klaus did not get on anyone's nerves is significant. He seems to have had some influence on his companions already for he used to intervene when they were getting out of hand, and encouraged them to do the right thing; Rorer adds that while still 'a very young boy' Klaus fasted every Friday.

At this very time at Domremy in Lorraine, a young peasant girl was being prepared for a mission as important in the history of France as that of Klaus in the history of Switzerland. They have often been contrasted, but there is very much in which Joan and Klaus resemble one another. Wölflin's description of Klaus as an excellent child, well-behaved, obedient to his parents, and attentive to what was told him by his elders, truthful, kind and respectful towards everyone, reads very like the testimony concerning Joan made at her rehabilitation. She too would slip away to pray while the others were at play, and, like Klaus's friends, her companions soon realized there was something special about her. Joan is described as a girl of great heart, of unshakable physical and moral courage, a girl of clear intellect and strong will.

Klaus came of age to vote in 1432 – the year after St Joan of Arc ended her short, eventful life at the stake at Rouen. It says much for the education the children received from their parents that boys were considered sufficiently mature to take part in the local parliament (*Landsgemeinde*) when they were only fifteen. Family life was on the whole much richer then than now, and the children early acquired a sense of responsibility. Although the von Flües were relatively wealthy farmers Klaus will have come into touch with neighbours of all ranks for in Switzerland 'the ruling class has never attempted to seal itself off from the great mass of the people, or to desire for itself a different and superior way of life' (Russell). On Sunday afternoons and during the long winter evenings, he and the other youngsters had ample opportunity to listen to the grown-ups talking about their work, about local affairs, or about events in the neighbouring cantons and beyond. In the year Klaus was born the Great Schism of the West, which had been such a nightmare to the faithful, virtually came to an end with the election of Odo Colonna as Pope Martin V at the Council of Constance. On his way back to Italy after the Council the Pope visited Zurich and Bern; great hopes were put in him, but when he died in 1431 the wholesale reform, of which the Church was in such urgent need, had still not been undertaken. Klaus will have heard about this, just as he will have listened to discussions on politics and wars, for the early fifteenth century is the period when the League and its several members took the offensive. Sometimes the Confederates were successful, but sometimes they were not. There were things that worried the farmers of Obwalden, the rout of the men of Uri and Obwalden, among whom were relatives of Klaus, at Arbedo near Bellinzona in 1422, for instance, and even more the growing preponderance of the towns in the League. Perhaps already at this time, the peace-loving boy felt some uneasiness when he heard descriptions of the wars, for, as the Convention of Sempach clearly implies, a brutality far removed from Christian teaching was often present.

Seeds of a Vocation

When he was sixteen, Klaus saw in a vision a tall, stately tower in the Ranft, on the very spot where now his little house and chapel stand, that is to say, quite near his home, on the western slope of the gorge of the Melchaa. As a result of this vision, Klaus told Erni an der Halden that from his very youth, he had always in mind to seek to lead a solitary life, in other words to become a hermit. Klaus told his friend the vision and the resolution that had formed in his mind as a consequence of it; he did not say anything about his interpretation of it. From the goal it set before him, it seems that the tower was symbolic of himself – the romanesque tower of the chapel on the hill he knew so well is in all probability related to the form of the vision; it seems too that the site of the tower represented for him the site of his future hermitage, so that the vision symbolized that he would one day live as a hermit in the Ranft. Although this interpretation comes from Erni an der Halden's deposition, it undoubtedly must have come originally from Klaus. An der Halden surely did not invent, even with hindsight, such an interpretation. This moment in Klaus's life is an instance of something mentioned by Christopher Butler: 'Often in the history of holy men the child has played out in anticipation an act of the spirit which yet only became real when the mature person rediscovered his childish inspiration and endorsed it.'

There is no need to wonder why Klaus, with his yearning for a life of solitude given to prayer and mortification, did not enter one of the monasteries on the territory of the Confederates, if the vision of the tower meant so much to him. Klaus's vocation was definitely to the eremitical life, and the only monastery in the Confederation that could have given him what he longed for was the Charterhouse at Thorberg, between Bern and Burgdorf, founded in 1397 by Peter von Thorberg. But it is doubtful whether Klaus knew of Thorberg, and even if he had done so, the security afforded by the ordered life of the Charterhouse would not have been of sufficient weight to lead him away from that form of eremitical life, which he knew had been practised in the forests of Obwalden and Nidwalden, and which seemed to be what God wanted of him.

The vision of the tower was the first indication to Klaus of his definitive vocation. And yet . . . thirty-four years were to elapse before he followed it! During that time not only did he follow in the footsteps of his father as a farmer, but he even married, and accepted positions of responsibility in civil affairs. The suggestion that he had first of all to get out of his system a deep attachment to the things that meant so very much to an Obwaldner – the family farm, village and district politics – is a plausible one, but this can hardly have entered Klaus's own head, and cannot be given as an explanation why he delayed. The call to become a hermit was perhaps not so clear as to leave no room for doubt; perhaps it seemed to him so impossible that it remained his own secret and a hope for the future.

It is not known with whom, or even whether at all, Klaus discussed his vocation. Yet now, five centuries after the events, a providential guidance is discernible; the years spent among the people were an essential part of God's plan in the role He had destined Nicholas to play in the history of Switzerland. These years helped to make him known and loved. He was cheerful and friendly; from an example he used in later life to describe how attractive God sometimes makes prayer, it is clear he was no spoilsport and enjoyed the country folk dances. His experience as a soldier, as a judge, and as a farmer was to serve to make him influential in later life in a way that, humanly speaking, he would hardly have been had he gone into the woods at sixteen. His life as a husband and father of a large family, paradoxical as it may seem, is equivalent to the 'long probation in the monastery' which St Benedict's Rule expects to precede the eremitical life.

The increased severity of Klaus's fasting can probably be dated about the time of the vision of the tower. His childhood companions, after describing the Friday fasting, add that 'afterwards' he fasted four times a week; we know from his son, Hans, that the four days were Monday, Wednesday, Friday and Saturday. On those days, and in Lent, Klaus only ate once during the day, and then only a small piece of bread or a few dried pears, which the people of those days considered a delicacy. Rorer goes on to say that he did this secretly so as not to make a show of it, yet when he was spoken to about it, or even reproved by those who feared it would injure his health, he would answer God wanted it. Here at least he is certain of himself, or rather certain of what God wants of him, and his determined answer is characteristic. The demand of God seemed to go against common sense but Klaus knew already he had to obey, and his behaviour bears in germ the obedience to a much harder call to sacrifice, which would cut right across the texture of his life and seemingly oppose prudence and common sense to a far greater degree.

Among the Fleeting Things of the World

As the chronology of the events in Klaus's life during the years between his twentieth and his fiftieth year is not certain, it may be easiest to treat these years under different aspects, even though this will mean a certain amount of overlapping in dates. This method has the advantage of completing each separate picture of Klaus in various spheres of activity without, too seriously, harming the picture of the development of a remarkable personality, and without rendering the view of his growing union with God lopsided.

Conscripted for Service

In the fifteenth century, as now, there was conscription in Switzerland, though, unlike the situation of today when the army's task is purely defensive, Switzerland being neutral, in the early fifteenth century, in order to ensure absolute freedom of military and economic communications, the various confederates were on the aggressive, and, jealous of any apparent infringement of their hard-earned independence, were quick to rush to arms. War and fighting seemed to enkindle an enthusiasm which overcame any deficiency in numbers among this newly independent people, and it is widely admitted that from the battle of Sempach, 1386, which marked the triumph of infantry over cavalry, until the battle of Marignano, 1515, which marked the triumph of artillery over infantry, the Confederation was the greatest military power in Europe. St Nicholas's span of seventy years fell during this period when the Swiss armies were on top of the world.

When Klaus was first called up the causes of the fighting were complicated, and the war was at first a civil war between confederates. Maybe this helps to explain his behaviour, on which it is important to read what the contemporaries who knew him well had to say. Only from them can we get a view of the man as he was – and that view proves to be much more interesting, and more attractive, than the picture later biographers, considerably influenced by the ideas of their own epoch, have painted.

Klaus, and his father, formed part of the Obwalden contingent which took part in the first Zurich war in 1440. Briefly, the events leading up to it are as follows: Frederick VII, Count of Toggenburg, the last great feudal lord on the left bank of the Rhine, died in 1436 leaving no heir. During his life, to ensure peaceful possession, he had made somewhat contradictory agreements with Zurich (in 1400) and with Schwyz (in 1417). The territory neighbouring the lake of Zurich was, in a certain measure, necessary to both for food supplies, and they had sought to obtain a legal right to it. Dispute broke out at once on Frederick's death concerning the portion of his inheritance promised, at different times, to the two confederates. It would have been difficult to say who was in the right at first, but Zurich soon put itself in the wrong by closing its markets to the inhabitants of Schwyz and Glarus (with whom the Count had also had equivocal dealings). This economic blockade was particularly serious since, owing to that year's poor harvest, it would have led to misery and famine in these two districts. In the war that ensued the country cantons faced

Zurich; happily the war was short, and in December 1440 Zurich accepted the peace of Lucerne.

Three years later Klaus was again called up. All efforts to bring Zurich back into line had failed. It claimed independence, and rejected the idea of a Swiss state; it agreed with the Emperor, a Habsburg, the traditional enemy, when he refused to confirm the liberties of the Swiss; it promised the return of Argovia (occupied by the Confederates in 1415, and of strategic importance) and the formation of a new confederation to oppose the forest districts. On the other hand, besides their legitimate complaint against Zurich, the country districts were animated by their ever-present suspicions of a town, and these certainly lent extra colour to their grievance and added violence to their warfare.

In May 1443 the Obwalden contingent, with that of Lucerne, stormed the Hirzel, driving back the Zurich troops. Then they went back home for the hay-making, to return two months later to take part in the battle of St Jakob an der Sihl. During this engagement, Stüssi, Zurich's leader, was killed as a result of a ruse in a mêlée before the town. Reasonable terms were made to a group of councillors, but when these returned to Zurich, the people, worked on by Austrian sympathizers, beheaded them as traitors. The country cantons, infuriated at this action, attacked Greifensee and massacred the inhabitants by way of reprisal, and once more laid siege to Zurich for the imperial help was not adequate to relieve the town.

Appealed to for help by the Emperor in 1444, Charles VII of France sent an army of 30,000 Armagnac freelances under the dauphin, Louis, against the Confederates. A small body of between 1,300 and 1,500 Swiss desperately resisted their advance at St Jakob an der Birs near Basle, on 26

August. Although the Swiss were cut to pieces and only 200 of them remained alive, the tremendous losses of the attackers forced them to sue for peace. Zurich's reluctance to abandon the Austrian alliance, as the Confederates demanded, caused the war to drag on until March 1446, when the heavy defeat of the Austrians at Ragaz rendered the alliance fruitless. The peace treaty, signed at Einsiedeln in 1450, settled by compromise the legal question which had so long been a cause of division. The Toggenburg itself, which passed now to a relative of the deceased count, was purchased before the end of the century by the Abbey of St Gall.

In all these battles in which an Obwalden contingent fought, Klaus took part. Recording in his diary the visit to Brother Klaus in the Ranft in 1474, Hans von Waldheim noted that Klaus had fought in several important actions. The rank of captain, often accorded him by biographers, is mentioned first by Gundelfingen of Constance. Although he wrote as early as 1488, this Canon of Beromunster is inaccurate about Klaus's peacetime career, and consequently what he had to say about the military career can hardly be treated as trustworthy either.

What did Klaus think of these wars? What did he feel about the ruse which brought about Stüssi's death? Did he share the opinion of many of his countrymen that the slaughter of almost the entire army outside Basle was a punishment for the savagery of the Confederates at Greifensee? Perhaps Klaus's attitude to war, as described by his companions, and his action at Diessenhofen in 1460 provide answers to these questions.

Wölflin, who usually did little more than faithfully paraphrase the Sachseln Kirchenbuch, seems to have been somewhat surprised by what he read there of Klaus at war.

Some later biographers have presumed to change that testimony quite radically; Wölflin however wrote:

> Klaus only took part in wars at the command of the authorities [this suffices to reject the identification of Klaus with a soldier of a somewhat similar name who took part, as a volunteer, in the relief of Nuremberg in 1450]. Although he was the greatest friend of peace, yet when it was a question of fighting for his country he did not want the enemy, on account of his inactivity, to be able to boast insolently; but as soon as the enemy was overcome he steadfastly admonished that they were to be spared.

The Kirchenbuch entries are certainly more unexpected. An der Halden recorded that Klaus 'did but little harm to the enemy, but rather did all he could to protect them'. Rorer said: 'In wars he did but little harm to the enemy, but rather always went to one side, prayed and protected them (the enemy) as much as he could.' These statements sound so incredible of a Swiss of that time that were they not made so soon after Klaus's death, and by two men who had known him so long, they could hardly be accepted. The two witnesses are certainly worthy of credence; an der Halden had been the Unterwalden bailiff (*Landvogt*) in Thurgovia, and Rorer had represented the parish in various disputes. From a comparison with Wölflin, it is clear that the protection Klaus extended to the enemy came after the battle. Rorer's statement then could be rendered: 'During a campaign Klaus preferred to pray than to fight, and after the battle he protected the defeated foe as best he could.' The protection of course meant protection from death, since the Confederates took no prisoners, simply doing away with any of the enemy who survived the battle. Klaus then opposed this brutal custom as far as he possibly could. Long before Henri Dunant founded the Red Cross, St Nicholas of Flüe was energetically standing up for the rights of prisoners of war, and he must be considered a patron and forerunner of that great work of mercy. A few decades earlier Joan had been moved by the treatment of prisoners. When she saw an English prisoner brutally and fatally struck on the head by the Frenchman in charge of a convoy of English prisoners, she got down from her horse, supported his head herself and comforted him to the best of her power. When asked why she always marched with a banner in her hand, Joan replied: 'Because I do not wish to use my sword, nor to kill anyone.'

The more one reflects on Klaus's behaviour during these campaigns the more one is amazed at what he got away with. The moral ascendancy of this young mountain farmer must have been such that however coarse and brutal the soldiery could be it yet recognized the deep goodness of their fellow conscript, and let him take part in the wars in his own way. An incident that probably took place during the war against the Austrians in 1460 illustrates admirably the moderating influence Klaus was able to exert. Joh. Joachim Eichorn, attached to the Ranft chapel in the seventeenth century, collector and editor of much precious information about Nicholas, records an incident at Diessenhofen. Doubt was cast on its authenticity by Durrer, but since the early Swiss military campaigns have been studied more closely that doubt seems no longer justified.

This campaign of 1460 brings the well-known Cardinal Nicholas of Cusa, Bishop of Brixen, indirectly into Klaus's life; it was as a consequence of the quarrel between the bishop and Sigismund, Duke of Austria and Count of Tyrol, that Pope Pius II excommunicated the duke. The Pope resorted to this step when his attempts at conciliation were answered by an armed attack on the cardinal, whose clumsy and somewhat abrupt efforts for monastic reform had been obstructed by the duke. Sigismund appealed from Pius to a future pope or a future council; Pius, however, called for the enforcement of the interdict under which he had placed Sigismund's dominions. The Swiss, who had taken Rapperswil from the duke in 1458, asked for nothing better than to occupy the whole of Thurgovia. Their leaders must have been aware how little justice they had on their side, and that they were 'obeying' the pope in this purely political matter only because it suited them, but there is no need to be surprised at Klaus's participation in such a war, for the majority of the people will have been easily convinced of the righteousness of the cause, if only by contrasting Nicholas of Cusa, a reforming bishop, and Sigismund, whose reputation was something of a byword.

Klaus was forty-three and father of several children when hostilities began in September 1460. The Swiss met with little resistance, but near Diessenhofen on the Rhine the Austrian garrison withdrew into the Dominican convent of St Katharinental. To drive them out the Swiss decided to set fire to the convent. Klaus heard of the decision and, after a prayer in front of a crucifix, went to the commanding officers and entreated them to desist from their intention. Their action would have been against the Convention of Sempach, and Klaus could certainly demand a withdrawal of the order on that ground alone. He assured the officers that the enemy would evacuate in three days, and that much good would still be done in the convent. The officers withdrew the order and Klaus himself brought the counter-order in time to save the church and convent to which the soldiers had already started to set fire. For another 400 years this convent was a house of fervent prayer; right up to the time of the suppression, in 1869, by the radical cantonal government of Thurgovia the nuns venerated Klaus as the saviour of their house, and during those 400 years the cross before which he had prayed was a precious relic.

Even were this incident legendary and not historical, as Durrer supposed on grounds which now seem without foundation, it would remain of inestimable value. The significance of an historical personage stands out not only from historical facts but also, and perhaps as much, from the picture drawn by contemporaries and the immediately following generations. Klaus stands out supremely as a man of peace, even when he was obliged to take part in wars, both from the evidence of Rorer and An der Halden and from the tradition of the Dominican nuns at St Katharinental – evidence and tradition are in perfect harmony with each other.

A Wife and Family

Probably in the late autumn of 1446 or early in 1447 Klaus married. His bride, Dorothea Wyss, from Oberwilen on the other side of the Lake of Sarnen, was much younger than he, but this pretty girl, whose looks Hans von Waldheim admired in 1474, proved an ideal companion. Since a parish priest, Kaspar Helwig of Siebenbürgen, was appointed to Sachseln on 30 May 1446, after a vacancy of thirty years, their marriage was probably blessed there.

As we have seen, An der Halden said that from the age of sixteen Klaus had always in mind to become a hermit. This marriage then presents a real problem, since it, more than anything else he undertook, put an enormous obstacle in the way of such a vocation. It seems more than likely that since his eremitical vocation was not unmistakably clear to him he felt bound to follow his parents' wishes, and they most probably intended him, the eldest son, not only to administer the family estate, but also to marry and continue the family line. This explanation fits in with his subsequent story, and throws light on the seeds of an inner conflict.

If we think a 'love-match' is the ideal then the suggestion that Klaus married because his parents wanted him to do so must sound deplorable. Yet a marriage of a man and woman who deeply cherish and respect one another, even though the element of 'being in love' is not present, is far preferable to one based uniquely upon romantic attraction. The strength of a marriage lies in selfless, enduring love bestowed for the increasing of the life of the beloved, a love which was for St Paul the symbol of the love of Christ and the Church.

The house Klaus built for his wife and family is somewhat smaller than his parents' home, but it is a fair-sized building, and, both in its dimensions and its walls, is preserved today as it was 500 years ago. Probably in 1447, Hans, the first child of a supremely happy marriage, was born. Hemma, who died in 1455, must certainly have seen others of the four boys and five girls who followed Hans into the world. Wölflin said this great blessing of ten children was a reward for absolute marital fidelity, which not even a misplaced word was allowed to assail. Durrer traced the fortunes of some of the children. Both Hans and Walter, the two sons who made depositions about their father after his death, filled the office of *Landamman* on several occasions, while Nicholas, the youngest, studied at the Universities of Basle and Paris, and was appointed parish priest of Sachseln in 1502, where he died after less than a year, to the deep regret of the parish. The parishioners had gone on a pilgrimage to ask God to restore him to health when news was brought them that he had died. Of the three daughters whose marriages are known, two, Verena and Dorothea, found husbands in Nidwalden, near the home of Klaus's mother –

an indication of the contact Hemma and her children kept up with the family at Altsellen in Wolfenschiessen. Konrad Scheuber, Dorothea's son, resembled his grandfather in many ways: after being *Landamman* of Nidwalden in 1543, he left his wife and two daughters, and, at the age of sixty, became a hermit. He settled at first in the Ranft, but was so disturbed by pilgrims keen on talking to Klaus's grandson that he retired to his own village and built a little hermitage above Wolfenschiessen.

Like all the Obwalden villages and townships, Sachseln had considerable alpine pastureland, permitting extensive stock breeding. Klaus owned the Bergmatt, on the Kernser side of the Melchtal, and, on the steep rocky slopes of the Klisterberg, a little alp known as the Klisterli. With modern methods of production and cultivation this property would easily be adequate for wintering a herd of thirty head of cattle, but development was not so intensive in the fifteenth century, and transport facilities, or rather lack of them, and the conditions of the roads made far greater demands on time and energy. We can get some idea of Klaus's work if we reflect on what was asked of a farmer whose pasturelands were at a distance from each other of some five miles as the crow flies, and at a difference of altitude of over 2,400 feet.

The family life of the von Flües was an intensely Christian one, constantly sanctified by prayer, just as is true of many of the families in Obwalden today. Klaus did not give up either his fasting or his assiduity in prayer. Dorothea probably wished sometimes that her husband enjoyed her cooking a little more, but Hans relates that his father fasted four times a week, and since that fasting was to be freer from the things of the world, it is unlikely his dinners on the remaining three days meant much to him. As for his prayer, Hans said that if at night he woke he heard his father, up and near the stove praying. Had the family a crucifix near the stove? Or is Durrer right in suggesting this can only refer to the winter, since in summer either Klaus or his eldest son would have been on the alpine pasturelands? During the day too, Klaus would often pray as he went along to the fields, and when there he would sometimes sit and pray.

Hans said that his father was caused much suffering and annoyance by the devil, and he described in particular one mishap. He had gone with his father to the Bergmatt, and while he was tending the cattle, his father rooted out the brambles to clean up the field. Suddenly the devil came and threw Klaus down the slope through a thicket for about thirty paces, so that he lost consciousness. Hans went to him, and picking him up, carried him into the chalet to the fire. When he came to, after some long time, although he was considerably injured, he remained quite patient, and only said: 'Now then, in God's Name, how the devil has maltreated me! Yet perhaps God wanted it so.' An der Halden also mentions this incident, and says that he saw the traces of the accident on Klaus's body. If the friend saw them, Dorothea surely saw them too – Hans must have told his mother about the fall in any case; with the sources silent on the point, we cannot know for certain whether Klaus and Dorothea talked about these happenings, but it would be strange if he did not tell her, as he told Rorer, that Our Lady was a source of comfort to him after these diabolic attacks.

There were happenings of another sort too, for Klaus's prayer was occasionally accompanied by imaginative visions. Unlike the vision of the tower, Klaus's later visions are not dated, but one of them surely belongs in this context, and helps to portray Klaus as he then was. Inevitably its imagery is adapted to the farmer's world. It may be as well to point out that sensible and imaginative visions are quite secondary in the spiritual life, and are hard to distinguish from similar phenomena, pathological or diabolic. Yet these graces, secondary as they are, do sometimes reveal precious graces which they either prepare or accompany.

Wölflin relates the following vision immediately after the incident with the devil on the Bergmatt. Klaus had come out to the fields to make sure that all was well with the cattle. There he sat down and began, as usual, to pray with all his heart, and to ponder prayerfully about heavenly things. Suddenly he saw a white lily growing out of his mouth; the lily had a quite wonderful scent, and stretched up into the sky. Soon the herd passed in front of him; for a moment he lowered his gaze, and looked at his horse, a more splendid beast than the rest. At once he noticed the lily bent down towards the horse, and was then eaten up by the animal. Wölflin gave two explanations; as a consequence of the vision, he wrote, Klaus realized we cannot attain to heavenly things while we still have a longing for earthly happiness; further, he understood that heavenly gifts are choked, just like the seed of the word of God which fell among thorns, when mixed up with the cares and worries of this world. In charming imagery, the vision presented a fundamental truth which must be known for our path to God: the tiniest complacency in oneself or in one's possessions, the tiniest breach of poverty of spirit, even in what concerns spiritual things, tarnishes the purity of our souls. There is no question here of sin, but simply of a lack of detachment from created things to be free to follow God. The obvious interpretation of this vision can only be fully understood in the light of the teaching of the great mystics, but how perfectly Klaus himself understood it can be judged from the following prayer:

25

My Lord and my God, take me from myself
and give me to Thyself as wholly Thine.
My Lord and my God, take from me all that
hinders my coming to Thee.
My Lord and my God, give to me all that
favours my coming to Thee.

Matters concerning Governing

Klaus belonged, as a freeholder, to a class of society with access to responsible positions in local government. His father had been active in local affairs and had set the example, so that it does not come as a surprise to hear that Klaus told a Dominican, who visited him in the Ranft, that he had had considerable authority as a judge and as a councillor, and in matters concerning the government of his homeland. 'Considerable authority' seems adequately to render *'fui potens in judicio* etc.', *'potens'* implying more than just ordinary activity. Heinrich von Flüe's name appears on official documents of 1437, 1442 and 1457. This last, connected with a tithe dispute, is especially interesting since it bears the names of both father and son: Heinrich figures as a witness and Klaus as a representative of the parish of Sachseln.

Only three documents survive with indications of Klaus's civic activity and these would in themselves certainly not warrant an assertion that he was very active in political affairs. Against this must be set Klaus's own categorical statement. The lack of greater documentary evidence is explained by Durrer, who pointed out that the lists of councillors and witnesses between 1442 and 1467 are missing from the Obwalden archives. This makes it difficult then to describe an important aspect of Klaus's life during these years. A certain amount can be read into the few documents and statements, and Heinrich Federer drew conclusions, in part from Klaus's influence in political matters in the later years of his life, in part, on the basis of heredity, from the political and diplomatic talents of his descendants. One thing is quite certain: Klaus deeply impressed his fellow citizens by his competence and, probably even more, by his selfless administration and devotedness. Federer suspected that his commanding appearance had something to do with his initial success. From Klaus's attitude during the last years of his life, it seems quite safe to conclude that already now he stood head and shoulders above the petty politics of his time, concerned as they chiefly were with the narrow interests of the district and canton. He must have realized how difficult government could be, when it depended on the democratic votes of farmers and communities with possibly only one-sided information. Yet he accepted posts of responsibility on behalf of the Sachseln community, and although not belonging to a family which then moved among the 'governing circles' he was quickly to the fore.

A rapid glance at two of the documents with Klaus's name will provide a glimpse of another aspect of life in Obwalden in the fifteenth century. The benefice of Sachseln, like the other Obwalden benefices, had been for many years in the patronage of the Habsburgs. This often led to the nomination of priests who were unacquainted with local conditions; vexed by this, the inhabitants claimed, from 1415, the right to choose their own parochial clergy. In 1434 the Emperor acknowledged this right, but unhappily the acknowledgment remained a dead letter. This led to endless strife, with as one consequence the absence of any parish priest at all at Sachseln for thirty-one years. In 1446 the

Bishop of Constance made use of the right of devolution, and, as we have seen, appointed Kaspar Helwig to Sachseln. The revenue had become quite meagre in the meanwhile, and the newcomer, whom the parishioners regarded as an intruder because he was not their nominee, was so keen on getting all he could, including the tithe of pears and apples, that the dispute had as sequel the imprisonment of the parish priest and his resignation in 1455. This episode is one facet of the caesaropapism, taken over from the Habsburgs by the Confederates, which constantly made the bishop's reform efforts even more difficult than they already were; it is also a sign of the mutual distrust ever present between the Confederates and the 'foreigners' who had, for one reason or another, to live on their territory; so often a little tact and generosity on both sides would have smoothed over the difficulties. The obstinacy of the people of Obwalden, as well as their indignation, in matters touching their pockets – even when these matters concerned canon law – is well known. Federer gave a personal reminiscence from our own times, but he insisted too that under the influence of a selfless, really apostolic priest their generosity can be unlimited. Helwig's successor, Hans Knaber, wrongly informed of the source of the revenue of the benefice, in his turn, demanded the tithe of pears and apples. To settle the matter the parish brought it before the local court in 1457. Their case was in the hands of Klaus and Erni Rorer – it is interesting to see Klaus's name before that of the older man. After the parish priest, Hans Knaber, had made his statement, Klaus von Flüe and Erni Rorer gave their version. They listed all the tithes of pears and apples, including those which had been bought out. In conclusion of the case, men of standing and good memory were called on to testify to the position; the first of those to affirm it on oath was Klaus's father. The court decided that the priest was asking for too much.

In the above affair Klaus represented the parish of Sachseln. In a document of 1459 he appears as a member of the Amman's tribunal, that is to say, as one of the cantonal law officers. Of rather more consequence is his appearance as the representative of Obwalden in 1462 at a meeting at Stans, to adjudicate in a dispute between the monastery of Engelberg and the parishioners of Stans, concerning the nomination of the parish priest. The patronage of Stans had belonged to the family of Regensberg-Seldenbüren; Konrad von Seldenbüren, the founder of Engelberg, had presented it to the monastery. The abbey had thus the right both to nominate a priest to look after the parish and to appropriate the revenue of the church. The consequences were not always very happy, and the parishioners strove to get priests of their own choosing. Representatives of the districts which carried out the administration of the monastery property sat in council with the parishioners; a solution, not according to canon law, but in keeping with the age was found: Stans was to choose its own parish priest, and present him to the abbot, who would propose him to the bishop for induction.

More interesting than these documents are the statements of Klaus's friends and of his son, Hans, concerning his attitude towards honours. Rorer, who is most explicit, said that Klaus withdrew from the world as much as he could, that he fled from and despised all temporal honours, and above all expended much energy to prevent himself becoming *Landamman,* which otherwise he would have become in due course. Rorer certainly implies that Klaus, despite his deep-seated disdain for temporal honours, accepted responsible posts, for in emphasizing that Klaus avoided becoming *Landamman* he makes it plain Klaus occupied the posts which were the stepping stones to the highest honour.

This refusal to accept the highest dignity the canton could offer is something quite out of the ordinary for a Swiss in any age, but in those first centuries of independence it is even more surprising. Klaus had perhaps been encouraged to accept the offices of judge and councillor because his fellow parishioners had asked him to represent them in court and in council, and because it seemed to be his duty. To accept the vote of the whole canton to be its head was quite another matter. Perhaps he had seen enough of the difficulties, encountered by the *Landamman*, and was acutely conscious how difficult it would be for someone who could not read printed documents to keep abreast of the situation. These and similar considerations mentioned by Federer are however not the reason for the refusal given by Rorer. Klaus does not seem to have been infected with the prevalent political ambition, and seems to have been vividly aware of the dangers attached to exalted positions, but he accepted jobs he could not conscientiously avoid. His attitude, of course, did not prevent him carrying out his duties with great care and zeal. He could say in all simplicity to his Dominican visitor that he did not remember ever having departed from the path of justice or having been an accepter of persons.

About 1465 Klaus withdrew from his functions as judge and councillor. Once more we are uncertain of the reason for an important step in his life. Neither Wölflin nor the witnesses of the Parish Register say much about Klaus's giving-up of his civic duties; it is possible to read into them the suggestion that it was to have more time for prayer. Other writers (from across the narrow Unterwalden confines) speak quite forcibly of a difference of opinion between Klaus and the other judges and councillors, so that the silence of the official biographer and the local friends may spring from a desire not to perpetuate differences between the authorities and a man, who, even in his lifetime, was revered as a saint. Popular tradition went so far as to say Klaus saw flames coming from the mouth of the unjust judges whose sentence he was unable to influence. Another source implies his opposition to the granting of citizenship (i.e. naturalization) for money and questionable influence when the candidates were not known to be honest, or were mixed up with dangerous commercial enterprises. In 1465 Unterwalden did grant citizenship to two German 'financiers' – Rudolf Motteli and his son Jakob. Klaus was clear-sighted enough to have seen through these men, whose machinations were to do harm to the Unterwaldners, blinded in 1465 by the Motteli wealth. Whatever the cause of his withdrawal from civic duties Klaus seems thereby to have made enemies. This is hardly surprising for in every age the thought is true, which Langland, in his 'Vision of Piers Plowman' put so succinctly a century earlier: '. . . as the way of the world is with the powerful, He who tells the truth is blamed the soonest.' If Klaus's opposition was on the question of the granting of citizenship to undesirable wealthy foreigners, as has been conjectured, it is cheering to note that, although he was no longer present among the councillors, his ideas on the subject eventually won the day. In 1478 Obwalden legislated to make naturalization more difficult.

All that Klaus had seen and learnt in civic affairs of human cupidity and blind self-seeking finds expression in one of his visions, and, although it probably belongs to the period after he had given up his functions as judge, it is well to set it here because it so admirably sums up Klaus's sentiments on the earthy ambition of many of his contemporaries. It is the second of the three visions described in a manuscript of 1480 discovered at Lucerne. The copyist – he signs himself Casparus am Buel de Unterwalden – seems to have made use of a text possibly written at Klaus's dictation; its style is both awkward and fascinatingly naive. Klaus was at this time getting up at midnight to meditate on the Passion of Our Lord, and it is legitimate to suppose this 'vision' may have been a dream.

There was a man who broke his sleep for love of God and for love of His passion. He thanked God for His Passion and His Martyrdom. And God gave him grace so that he found both pleasure and delight therein. After that he laid himself down to rest, and it seemed to him in his sleep or in spirit that he came to a square in a village. There he saw a great many people, doing much hard work and yet still very poor. And he stood and stared at them, and he was puzzled that they were working so hard and were nevertheless so poor. Then on his right he saw appear a tabernacle, and it was beautifully built. Therein he saw an open door at the entrance, and he thought to himself: you must go into the tabernacle, and must see what there is inside, and must soon go in through the door. There he came to a kitchen belonging to the whole village. Then he saw on his right a staircase, perhaps about four steps high. There he saw some people go up, but only a few. It seemed to him that their clothes were speckled a little with white, and he saw a spring close to the steps flowing in a great trough towards the kitchen; it was composed of three things: wine, oil and honey. And the spring flowed so rapidly that it was like the glittering which sun rays give forth, and it babbled so noisily that the mansion resounded loudly as from the blowing of a horn. And he thought: you must go up those steps and see whence comes that spring. And he wondered greatly that, being so poor, nobody went to draw from the spring, which they would after all have been quite free to do, since it was common property. And he went up the steps and entered a large hall. Then he saw in the middle of the hall a big four-cornered chest whence gushed the spring. And he made towards the chest to look at it. And as he went towards the chest, he seemed to be sinking down, as one walking across a marsh, and he quickly drew up his feet and reached the chest. And he knew in spirit that he who does not quickly raise his feet cannot reach the chest. The chest was strengthened at its four corners with four mighty iron clasps. The spring flowed away through a pipe and it resounded both inside the chest and inside the pipe in such beautiful wise that he wondered greatly thereat. The spring was so clear that one might easily have perceived a man's hair on the bottom. And although it gushed out so abundantly still the chest remained full to the brim, so that it overflowed. In spirit he understood that no matter how much flowed out, yet could it still have contained even more, and he saw it trickling out through all the cracks. And he thought: you had better go down again. Then he saw that it continued to flow abundantly into the trough, and he thought to himself: you will go out into the open and see what those people are doing and why they do not enter and draw from the spring, since there is such an abundance; and he went out of the door. There he saw those people doing heavy work, and with all that yet they were very poor. Then he watched them closely to see what they were doing. There he saw a man, who had made a fence right across the square; in the middle of the fence he had made a gate, keeping it closed and saying: I will let you go neither this way nor that unless you pay me a penny. He saw another man standing there, wielding a club and saying: this had been invented to make you hand over a penny to me. He saw pipers piping to the people and demanding a penny from them. He saw tailors and shoemakers and all kinds of craftsmen, all wanting a penny from him. And although they were so busy doing these things, because they were so poor, yet they hardly received anything. And he saw nobody enter to draw from the spring. And while he stood there, looking at them, the surrounding countryside changed, and became wild and desolate, and resembled the tract of country round about Brother Klaus's chapel, where he had his dwelling-place, and he knew in his spirit the tabernacle to be Brother Klaus himself.

Primarily this vision has to do with the mystery of the Trinity, infinitely loving in its offer to communicate by grace the divine life to men – an offer which so very many do not heed because they are so preoccupied with material wealth. The crystal clear three-fold fountain is a symbol of the Holy Trinity found elsewhere in the German mystics, but the idea that he himself is the tabernacle through which the fountain flows is unique. Many biographers, perhaps embarrassed by them, declare that these last words are those of an enthusiastic admirer and not Klaus's own, or they omit them from their version of the vision. Yet they are not an offence against humility, any more than the Blessed Virgin's words in the Magnificat imply pride in her; they indicate a consciousness of a role to be played in God's plan, apparent already in the vision of the tower. Klaus does not suggest that he is the fountain, but that he is the place where the fountain will communicate itself.

It is not pride to recognise the gifts God has freely lavished on one, to have a presentiment of gifts to come, to foresee the mission God will invest one with, provided there is no complacency in oneself but only in the giver, who freely chooses both the subjects and the instruments of his mercy. However much humility and magnanimity may differ they are not mutually exclusive; they are rather compatible and complementary being equally necessary for the harmonious perfection of the divinised soul. (Benoit Lavaud)

In Search of a Way

On 30 August 1459, the church of Sachseln was reconciled. This means that the church had been under an interdict, and maybe the leading members of the parish had also been envisaged by the sentence, perhaps as a result of the disputes with Helwig and Knaber In 1460, Hans Burkard of Lenxingen, a native of the canton of Bern, became parish priest of Sachseln. To two holders of the benefice, who had seemed to the parishioners far too fond of fruit, there succeeded a man who is suspected of having failed in another direction, and of having become, quite literally, father to at least one of his parishioners. Not once is there mention of any relations between him and Klaus, although he was parish priest for twenty-four years.

With such priests in the parish, Klaus might well have lacked respect for the clergy, but, like St Catherine of Siena a century earlier, he unerringly distinguished the person from the office. What he had to say about this is very interesting. 'More than all other men,' he told the Dominican who visited him in 1469, 'I loved and honoured priests, so much so that whenever I saw a priest it seemed to me that I saw an angel of God.' According to this same Dominican, Klaus considered that his great veneration and devotion for the sacrament of the Body and Blood of Jesus Christ was a result of his respect for priests. This order of things is unexpected – for St Catherine of Siena, it was that very sacrament of which he was the minister that made even an unworthy priest, Pietro of Semignano, dear to her – and it seems to suggest an early influence in his life seeking to remedy or forestall the effect on him of a clergy which was not always a source of edification.

Among the clergy, Klaus had, already at this time, one

very good friend. Heinrich am Grund and his father, probably sprung from Obwalden stock since the name is not met elsewhere, were accorded citizenship of Lucerne in 1449. On 2 May 1465, Heinrich was named parish priest of Kriens. This 'devout priest of Lucerne', as Klaus called him, helped Klaus considerably at a critical moment. The intimacy mentioned by Klaus seems to suggest they had been friends for some years, but, tantalizingly, the exact date of this crisis in Klaus's life is unknown.

'God sent me a grievous trial,' Klaus told the Dominican visitor, 'of such a nature that it did not let me rest either day or night; I was so very grievously upset that even life with my darling wife was a burden, as was the companionship of my children.' These symptoms – restlessness with no apparent reason and an antipathy towards his nearest and dearest – seem to indicate a state of melancholia, or perhaps rather an acute case of loss of self-confidence, but Klaus gave no reason for the state of mind, and he does not seem to have known of one. He was forty-five or thereabouts, the age at which it has been said 'a man begins to doubt whether he has really followed his true vocation, really run his life on the right lines' (Yves Congar): but it would be far from true to say that his life, exteriorly at least, was something of a failure.

It seems hard to exaggerate the importance, for understanding Klaus, of this Dominican's memoir. From it comes the information about his political and civic life, and now in and between these lines much of the drama of his soul can be read. The years of married life, of close companionship with a woman whom he loved deeply – Klaus's devotion to the Blessed Virgin Mary is a clue to his respect for all women and especially for his wife – the years of working his own land, land which he would inherit and which in his turn he would pass on to his children, the years of activity in 'matters of the fatherland', had not stifled the vocation that he had believed to be his when he was sixteen; probably most of the time it was far from his conscious thinking, but the life he was leading could not ultimately satisfy his longing.

> 'While I was in this condition,' Klaus went on, 'the person I mentioned [Heinrich am Grund], with whom I was on particularly intimate terms, came out to have a tête-a-tête with me. As we chatted about various things I told him about the anxiety I felt and the depression I was going through. Whereupon he proffered much good advice and suggested remedies by which he hoped to lighten my trial, but I told him I had tried them and their like without finding any relief, nor had they been any use at all. Then, finally he said there remained one last excellent and most profitable remedy, namely, the devout meditation of the Passion of Jesus Christ. Whereupon, extremely relieved, I replied that I was unaware of it, and that I did not know the manner and form of meditating on the Passion of Jesus Christ. So he taught me the points of the Passion dividing them up according to the seven canonical hours.'

Every hermit, indeed every contemplative (and Klaus was a contemplative before he became a hermit) needs to find a way which is for him/her uniquely relevant. The 'way' will be found to be more effective than the method of prayer often recommended. The words of Isaiah 'This is your way, follow it' are heeded and the contemplative, be it, for example the Russian pilgrim or St Teresa of Lisieux, with her 'little way', will follow that way towards an ever closer union with the Beloved. Am Grund has guided Klaus now to his way, which Dom Doyère aptly called 'Passion-mysticism.'

At that period there were already in circulation several popular devotional books for meditating on the Passion according to the seven canonical hours. They provided, as it were, a breviary for lay folk, indicating a phase of the suffering of Christ on which to meditate at each of the hours when the public prayer of the Church was offered by priests and monks and nuns, and giving prayers which were easy to memorize. It seems that although Klaus was able to read letters and charters, he could not read books, otherwise Heinrich am Grund would simply have provided him with a book from his own well-stocked library, instead of himself initiating Klaus into the form of prayer.

The division of the Passion according to the hours is not exactly the same in all these books so that we can no longer be quite certain of the order in which Klaus meditated, but the differences are so slight that we can get a good idea of his prayer by following the work most widespread at the time. The second part of the *Speculum humanae salvationis* (Mirror of Man's Redemption) contains such a meditation, divided up according to the seven canonical hours, with pictures illustrating each section. For two years, at least, this formed the most important part of Klaus's day, so that some details must be given.

At each canonical hour Klaus gave thanks to Our Lord Jesus Christ, his God and his Saviour, for the love he had shown for him in one particular aspect of the Passion; the particular point led up then to a petition for a virtue or grace usually corresponding to the point that had been meditated on. About six o'clock in the evening, for the hour of Vespers, Klaus thanked Christ for the love shown when he put before Klaus an example of most perfect humility, washing the disciples' feet, and not refusing even to wash and dry the feet of the traitor. Quite naturally there followed a prayer for true and perfect humility. Then too he thanked for the ineffable love shown in the institution of the sacrament of Christ's body and blood, and he prayed for the grace to be strengthened at the hour of his death and to be brought happily to Christ's presence by this sacrament. At the hour of Compline, the Church's official night-prayer, Klaus thanked for the love that Our Lord Jesus Christ had shown by the agony in the garden, for the loving meekness He showed there when He did not withhold His lips from the traitor's kiss, and allowed Himself to be bound; Klaus prayed to be freed from the chains of the evil one. Shortly after midnight, Klaus prayed his night office, his Matins, thanking Our Lord for the great love He had shown in allowing Himself to be mocked and spat upon in the house of Caiphas for Klaus's sake. He then prayed his most sweet Lord, by the blindfolding of his eyes, by the affronts He received when He was struck and spat upon, to forgive him, poor wretch that he was, the affronts of all the offences he had committed in His sight. Early in the morning, at the time of Prime, Klaus meditated on Christ's great patience in allowing Himself to be bandied between Pilate and Herod, and to be mocked by Herod and his soldiers, and he thanked Christ for the love which prompted this and he prayed his Lord to grant him true patience in all troubles, so that he might bear with adversity in this life in such a way that he merit to dwell for ever with Him in His kingdom. Then at nine, the hour of Terce, he thanked Our Lord for the love He had shown him in letting Himself be scourged and crowned with thorns, and he prayed that Jesus would deign so to scourge him, whether he liked it or not, in this world, that he would not deserve to be scourged in the next, not even to suffer the scourges of purgatory, but instead, to arrive without scourging at eternal glory. At midday, the hour of Sext, Klaus thanked for the love Jesus showed him in being sentenced to death, in carrying the cross and in being crucified for him, and for the very great love He showed in praying for His enemies. Klaus prayed that he too might enter the kingdom with his Lord. Finally at the time of None, three in the afternoon, he gave thanks to our Lord for His death, recalling Christ's words on the cross, and the opening of His side after death. He prayed to Christ, by His most bitter death, to grant him grace so to love Him and to serve Him as to merit, after this exile, to come to the glory of the blessed.

Klaus pulled himself together, and performed this devotion every day. It seems to have had the desired effect, for, as he put it, he made progress, according to his poor measure, through the mercy of our Redeemer. For someone who was suffering from depression it must have been excellent medicine to stop constantly turning round himself and his own troubles, and instead to turn to the sufferings of Christ, and to do so not just now and then but regularly and according to an exact order. Each time he thought of those sufferings Klaus expressed his gratitude for Christ's incomparable love not only for the whole world but even for him, Klaus, for the Passion was the supreme manifestation of that love. Constantly assuring himself of God's great love, and constantly expressing his thanks for it, must have brought relief to Klaus's low spirits.

His prayer was at this time seemingly full of consolation, and he was visibly strengthened by it. His relations with his tremendous Lover were becoming ever more intimate. Yet it was not long before Klaus came to the conclusion that, entangled as he was in various occupations and in worldly affairs, he was carrying out his devotions less fervently when he was in the company of others. And so he would frequently withdraw to the Ranft (to the Dominican he described it as 'this secret and nearby place of my passion') to pray.

Dorothea was the only one who knew of his going there, and even she only knew by accident. 'And thus I continued for two years...' Klaus said. At this point the Dominican's precious narrative comes abruptly to an end.

Klaus seems to say that it was in view of his prayer that he withdrew from worldly affairs; since he is chiefly speaking of his life of prayer, this need not be taken as contrary to the tradition of a break on account of a vehement difference of opinion between Klaus and his fellow councillors. He may have come to realize that he would have been carried out of himself (and perhaps already was terribly distracted) by excessive care had he attempted, any longer, to put forward his point of view in face of opposition. Enough is known of the pettiness of the politicians of the time to sense something of Klaus's suffering. There is little more painful for a passionate, sensitive nature than the continual inner indignation arising from seeing serious misbehaviour in those around one, particularly if they are the very people who should be setting an example. Events crowd in on one, and one's inner sanctuary is so beset that the only solution is to withdraw if one is not to lose oneself. This is surely what happened to Klaus. The vision of the lily may have helped him to decide his line of action. The circumstances of that vision imply Klaus would not let anything come in the way of his prayer at the appointed time. Two visions of this period, a vision of Christ coming to Klaus as a courteous lovable pilgrim and a vision symbolic of the 'gratitude' of God the Father, of the Blessed Virgin Mary, and of their Son for Klaus's love and devotion, show how much his thoughts were revolving round God's love for him and his love for God. However idiosyncratic their form, they are something to be shared and experienced, and are given here close to the original text.

And it seemed to him in his spirit that a man in pilgrim's garb came to him; in his hand he had a staff, he had attached his hat and arranged it to hang down behind as someone wishing to go out, and he wore a cloak. And in spirit he thought that he came from where the sun rises or from very far. And although he did not say so he came from the place where the sun rises in Summer. And see, he came towards him, he stood in front of him and sang this word: Allelula. And as he started to sing the country around took up his voice; the earth and all that is between heaven and earth sustained his voice, as little organs do large ones. And he heard as from a single source three perfect words, proceeding and then terminating so simultaneously, like a spring jumping back into its lock. And he heard three perfect words, for each one was separate and yet one could only speak of one word. And when he had ended his song he asked the man for a gift, and he found a penny in his hand and did not know whence it had come to him. And he took off his hat and received the penny in the hat. And the man had never realised that it was such a great honour to receive a gift in one's hat. It puzzled the man greatly who he was and whence he came; and he said 'I come from thence,' and no more; and he did not want to tell him any more. And he stood in front of him and looked at him. At that moment he transformed himself and let himself be seen bareheaded, and he wore a coat, which was blue or grey in colour, and he did not see the cloak any longer. And he was such a noble well-built man that he had nothing better to do than to look at him with exceeding pleasure and desire. His face was tanned which gave him a noble beauty. His eyes were black like a magnet, his limbs were so well formed that they gave him a special splendour. Although he was clothed in his garments, these did not prevent his limbs being seen. And while he looked without wearying at him, he turned his eyes on him. Then there appeared many great wonders: Mt.Pilatus sank down into the ground and the whole earth lay bare, so that it seemed to him that all sin that was in the world was made public. [The geographical position explains the mention of Mt. Pilatus since from Sachseln it effectually blocks the horizon and view towards the north-west.] And there appeared a great crowd of people and behind the people appeared the truth, and all of them had their face away from the truth. And a large tumour appeared on the heart of each one, like two fists together. And this tumour was egoism, which made these people err so much that they could not bear (to look into) the man's face any more than men can bear (to look into) flames of fire; and they went hither and thither in a wretchedly frightened state, cursing and misbehaving; and he saw them going right away. And the truth which appeared from behind, remained there. And his face was changed like a Veronica. [A 'Veronica' refers to the face of Christ preserved on a cloth, commonly called 'the veil of Veronica'.] He had a great longing to gaze yet more on him, as he had seen him before, only his clothes were changed, and he stood before him clothed in a bearskin, with trousers and a coat. And the bearskin was sprinkled with gold. But he saw and clearly recognised that it was a bearskin. The bearskin adorned him so remarkably well that the man both saw and said that it looked exceptionally becoming on him. And as he stood there before him and let himself be seen looking so noble in the bearskin, he felt that he wanted to take leave of him. He said to him: 'Where will you go?' He answered: 'I will go up into the country.' More than that he did not want to say. And as he took leave of him, he looked after him without growing weary. Then he saw that the bearskin glistened now more, now less, as if someone were handling well polished weapons and he were to see the glittering on the walls. And he thought that there was something hidden from him. And when he had left him for some four steps or so, he turned round and taking off his hat he bowed to him and took his leave. He then recognized the singular love that the man bore him, and he felt quite oppressed knowing that he did not deserve such love, and yet that the love was there. And he saw, in his spirit, his face and his eyes and his whole being full of loving humility like a bowl so brimful of honey, that it could not hold another drop. Then he did not see him any more. But he felt so completely satisfied that he did not yearn for any more. It seemed to him that he had made known to him all that there is in heaven and on earth.

The almost invariable use of the pronoun both for the pilgrim and for the visionary, as well as the occasional indiscriminate use of 'the man', make awkward reading but on the whole to whom these terms refer is clear enough. The translation of '*vol minricher demout*' by 'full of loving humility' is inadequate, but there is no word to render the old German word '*minne*', with all its wealth of meaning. It contains more than 'love'; the aspect of an intense loving concern, even of a kind of telepathy of soul with a beloved person now far away or even dead, is present. Its use here is significant; it shows the depths of Klaus's faith in, and awareness of, God's love. The pilgrim's humility, so 'rich in love', 'like a bowl so brimful of honey that it could not hold another drop', filled Klaus with a deep satisfaction. It seems clear that Klaus's feeling of having been taught all is connected with the sensation of love that flooded him and so filled all his yearning; with the poet's intuition Novalis saw something similar when he wrote, in a fascinating poem, of a time when 'those who sing or those who kiss will know more than all the great scholars.' (From the poem '*Wenn nicht mehr Zahlen*'.)

Because of the important role played by the Blessed Virgin Mary, one biographer (Fritz Blanke) found the third vision unorthodox, but it is quite in accord with traditional

Catholic piety, based on the definition of the Council of Ephesus (in 431) of Mary as Mother of God,

There was a man who broke his sleep for love of God and for love of His Passion and he thanked God for His Passion and martyrdom. And God gave him grace so that he found both pleasure and delight therein. After that he laid himself down to rest. And while his understanding was bound in chains and he thought that he was not asleep, it seemed to him that someone entered the door and, standing in the middle of the house, with a loud and joyful voice, called him just as he was named, saying, 'Come and look at your father and see what he is doing.' And it seemed to him that he came quickly to the extremity of a bow (i.e. as far as an arrow will go) to a beautiful tabernacle in the middle of a large hall. He saw some people living there, clad in white robes, and he who had called him was there; he stood by his side, presenting to him what he had to say as an advocate would. And although he spoke yet he did not see his countenance nor did he puzzle about it, and he presented him his speech and said 'This is he who has taken care and carried your son, and who came to his aid in his anguish and his need. Thank him, and thank him again and again.' Then there came a handsome, majestic man striding through the palace; his face shone brightly and he wore a white garment, like a priest in his alb. And he laid both arms on his shoulders and drew him to himself and thanked him with all the fervent love of his heart for having assisted his son and having helped him in his distress. And that same man felt overcome and quite awestruck and confessed himself unworthy, saying: 'I do not know that I have ever rendered a service to your son.' Then he left him and did not see him any more. And then there came a beautiful, valiant woman walking through the palace, also in a white garment of the same kind. And he saw well that the white garment was as becoming as though it were newly washed. And she laid both her arms on both his shoulders and pressed him firmly to her heart with an overflowing love for having so faithfully assisted her son in his distress. And the man was overcome with fear, saying: 'I do not know that I have ever rendered service to your son, except only that I have come here to see what you are doing.' Then she took leave of him and he saw her no more. Then he looked beside him. There he saw the son sitting beside him in a chair, and saw that he too had a similar garment on; it was flecked with scarlet, as though someone had directed a sprinkler at it. And the son bent towards him and thanked him deeply for his assistance in his great distress. Then he looked down at himself and saw that he too wore a white garment flecked with scarlet, just like the son. This surprised him greatly, not remembering having put it on. And at this very moment all at once he found himself at the same place where he had laid down, so that he did not think that he had slept at all. Amen.

M-L von Franz, in her thought-provoking, though sometimes exasperating, study of the visions of St Nicholas, said this vision suggested Klaus was unusually modest, and was very conscious of how far away from God he was; it brought him an answer to all his troubles, revealing to him that the darkness he was going through was willed by God and had as its end the divinization of a quite ordinary human being.

If Klaus really was acutely aware of his remoteness from God, this does not seem to have been incompatible with a firm conviction that he was ready to abandon himself unreservedly to God's will. To the three men, whose bearing and dress suggested nobility, who appeared to him while he was working at home one day, he said that he would surrender himself to none but God, and that he desired to be God's servant, body and soul.

Although the position was becoming clearer – he was praying now to become a hermit – it seems he was in one of those tragic situations where one strives desperately to do the right thing, and at the same time senses somehow that one is on the wrong track. Perhaps if the rest of the Dominican's narrative existed there would be no need to conjecture, but that is imperative as things stand.

The Supreme Sacrifice

Soon after Klaus had retired from public life, as he was going out one day to mow in the Melchtal, he prayed to God for the grace of 'a devout life'. From the context there can be little doubt that he meant the life of a hermit, or at very least someone living only for contemplation. At that moment, he later told Walter, his second son, a cloud came towards him from the sky, and spoke to him, saying that he should abandon himself to God's will, for he was a foolish man, and what God wanted to work with him, therein he too should be willing.

What Klaus heard from the cloud was certainly a reproach. He was being reproached for failing to cooperate decisively, for still hesitating before the last step. He had said to the three men that he was ready to be wholeheartedly God's servant. And yet this voice from the cloud seemed to suggest his petition was in the nature of an escape, a shifting of the responsibility from himself to God, and it revealed that he was, probably all unwittingly, deceiving himself. Dare one conjecture that Klaus had not yet envisaged the possibility of becoming a hermit while Dorothea still lived? One hesitates to suggest, that in his prayer to become a hermit, was almost implied the prayer for that last unmistakable sign that would no longer allow him to doubt, namely his wife's death. The vision of the cloud helped Klaus decisively to see that although he believed himself ready for anything he was fighting shy of the last sacrifice. Walter, after recording what his father had told him of the message from the cloud, added 'that was why he (Klaus) gave himself up completely to God's will.' Did Klaus now learn from am Grund that he could become a hermit while Dorothea still lived, if only she would give her consent? It seems to be very likely, and from this moment he was determined no longer to delay, but to do all that lay within his power to fulfill what he could no longer doubt was God's will for him.

Only one of the early documents describes Klaus's efforts to obtain Dorothea's consent, and even Wölflin is so short that but a scanty picture of the discussions emerges. Immediately after his version of the vision of the cloud, somewhat less vivid than Walter's, particularly in the nature of Klaus's petition which preceded it, Wölflin wrote: 'Then his fervour grew greater day by day; he was moved by the stimulus of divine grace to such a degree that the whole world seemed already to be inadequate for the dwelling-place of this chosen friend of God.' (Wölflin here probably had in mind St Gregory's comment on a vision of St Benedict, *Book of the Dialogues*, II, Ch. 35. 'All creation is small to the soul that sees the Creator. Though it catch but a glimpse of the light of God, all that is made becomes little in its eyes. By the light of that intimate vision the grasp of the mind is so extended and enlarged in God that it transcends the world. Nay, the soul of the seer transcends itself also, and becoming rapt above itself by the light of God is enlarged in its inmost being.' (The translation is Abbot Justin McCann's.))

And so he told his beloved wife what he had resolved, saying that he had made up his mind, having put aside the attractive things of the world to seek out some place in solitude fit only for a life of contemplation. For this to be lawful for him her permission was needed, so he tried to persuade her, urging chiefly this consideration that it was pointless for him once more to get entangled in domestic worries and through them to realise quite clearly that nothing at all of what mattered in his life corresponded in the least to a desire for a worldly career. [Wölflin's reason why Klaus wanted to go far afield has been given; the only other contemporary to give a reason is von Waldheim, who said that he planned to go as a pilgrim from one holy place to another; this can very well be complementary to Wölflin's reason.] Since again and again he besought her, she at last with much ado unwillingly gave her consent to his importunate entreaties.

Wölflin's few lines reveal something of the drama played out in the souls of husband and wife. It is clear that Dorothea opposed Klaus's project very strongly. She needed to be convinced that he was really being called by God before she would consent to what meant for her the destruction of their wedded love, and she struggled with all her being against it. Klaus's own anguish can easily be imagined, and he certainly had recourse to prayer as well as to argument and entreaty in trying to make her see things as he did. In the end he wrested the indispensable consent from her, but Dorothea surrendered unwillingly, and was rather worn down by her husband's persistence than convinced. Humanly speaking sympathy goes out rather to Dorothea than to Klaus, and it is not in the least surprising that some of his relatives opposed his plan. This very year his eldest son, Hans, married Elsbet of Eiwil, daughter of the *Landamman* and allied himself with an influential local family; his later career shows how much he had an eye to his political position and it is more than likely that he too opposed his father's proposal. Once Klaus had his wife's consent, however, he did not need to bother about the opposition of his relatives, and he prepared for the departure. Klaus presumably chose the middle of October for the final leave-taking, firstly so that he might have time to bring in the harvest and to see to all that was necessary for wintering the family's herd, and secondly to assure himself that all was well with Dorothea and little Nicholas, the youngest of their children, who had been born on 24 June.

Nothing is known of the last weeks they spent together, but it is not difficult to imagine the suffering of both Klaus and Dorothea. Although his wife had given her consent, it was an unwilling one and Klaus, though convinced God was calling him, must have felt keenly the suffering and anguish of the coming separation. To suggest otherwise would be to belittle the depth of their union. Saints are not stoics, impervious to joy and suffering – if anything they are more tender and more sensitive to suffering than others – and though God's grace gave Klaus and Dorothea the strength to separate it will not have done away with the acutely painful wrench that inevitably accompanies a definitive leave-taking.

On Friday, 16 October, St Gall's Day, 1467, Klaus left home. Klaus's leaving of his wife, which even in his lifetime provoked much discussion, still puzzles and even scandalizes so many, that it must be insisted it can only be judged aright if it is seen from a supernatural point of view, and seen as God's work. In the history of the Church, there are cases – admittedly very rare – where an imperious divine call urges a husband and wife to separate by common consent, to deprive themselves of each other, in order to be united to God more perfectly than they were when leaning on each other in their life together. The bond joining Christian husband and wife together can only be broken or modified by God, who blessed it originally. He alone, who, in the inscrutable ways of divine wisdom, sometimes allows this bond to be broken by death, when humanly speaking, its maintenance seems most necessary, can also loosen it in another way. He can call a married man, even if there are children, to leave his wife, in the midst of their happiness, provided that she consents and the education and future of the children are provided for. It was this call Klaus had heard. His decision to leave Dorothea would have been not only foolish but also seriously wrong had it sprung simply from his own initiative, but he was now convinced that its inspiration was from God, and, being convinced of that, he was bound to follow this extraordinary vocation.

Klaus then left Dorothea and their family and headed, not for the Ranft, but for 'foreign parts'. This turn of events comes as something of a surprise, for the Ranft was indicated as the place of his solitude as early as the vision of the tower when he was sixteen, as the place of his influence in the vision of the crystal-clear fountain, and, for some time, it had been to the Ranft that he had often repaired to meditate on the Passion. Wölflin gives the reason why Klaus went in the opposite direction, saying that he feared that if he made his hermitage in his homeland it would easily happen that his way of life would be attacked as a hypocritical showing-off by those who resented it. From the later opposition it is obvious that Klaus's fear was not unfounded. He knew his compatriots (or some of them) would not appreciate his plan to found a hermitage in their midst, and, even if Dorothea understood and agreed with him now – and that after all does not certainly follow from her reluctant consent – many of his relatives would not. The whole plan would seem eccentric or ridiculous to them, and because it was a relative of theirs, they would feel it cast aspersions on their own sanity and good sense.

Klaus had decided to go abroad where no one knew him, but no sooner had he crossed the Hauenstein Pass and thus the frontiers, as they then were, of the Confederation, than there came an extraordinary intervention in his scheme. As he neared Liestal, the little town appeared to Klaus to be all red. This ruddy appearance of the town may have been the result of an uneasy conscience, because Klaus was going away from the Ranft where he 'sensed' he belonged. Whatever the explanation, Klaus was frightened at the town's appearance and immediately changed his direction, going towards a farmhouse standing apart. The coincidence that it was the first town across the frontier which presented this forbidding aspect does not seem to have made Klaus change his mind at once, for after getting into conversation with the farmer, he told him of his plan. The splendid simplicity of Klaus's action does not deserve to go unnoticed. Bewildered and troubled, and sensing that he was too far off the track to find the way back alone, he decided quite simply to put the matter to this unknown farmer. The farmer seems to have been an outspoken, sensible person, who did not hesitate to say what he thought – Klaus's attitude must anyway have encouraged him to do so. He advised Klaus to go back to his own people, firstly because that would be more pleasing to God than being a burden to foreigners (he envisaged Klaus living on alms), and secondly because it would be more peaceful for Klaus, since not everyone was favourably disposed towards the Confederates. Klaus was impressed by this advice, but, instead of asking for hospitality for the night, he left the house at once. He went out into the fields, and laid down by a hedge to spend the night there.

When Klaus was asleep 'there came a brightness and a glow from heaven, which opened his stomach and gave him such pain that it seemed someone was cutting him up with a knife.' This incident under the hedge near Liestal, which both Rorer and am Grund recorded, had two effects on Klaus, of which the first to be apparent to him was the urge to get up immediately to 'return home to the Ranft, and serve God there', which, Rorer said, 'he did at once, in the morning'.

But he did not! Klaus got up from the hedge, and set off back homewards. If Hans von Waldheim's diary is accurate on the point, Klaus arrived back home, presumably in the late evening, and without speaking to any of the family, went into the stables to pass the night. Early in the morning he made off, so that when one or other of the family came to milk, there was no sign of the wanderer who had spent the night in the stable. Klaus will have had little to disturb his meditation on the Passion as he came back from Liestal, but, either then or during the night, it seems there was still a struggle going on in his soul. God had clearly let him see there could be no question of hiding his identity as an unknown hermit or pilgrim far away from home. But Klaus had not yet won through. It seems he was still haunted by the thought of what the neighbours would say; after all such opposition would be awkward for his wife and family too, so he could argue he was not thinking only of himself. It is not difficult to imagine his wondering and doubting whether it was really possible God wanted him in the Ranft, so very near home.

Eight days later some hunters came across Klaus on his own property in the Melchtal, on the forsaken Klisterli alp. The hunters told Peter von Flüe of Klaus's whereabouts, and seem to have spread the news locally. Peter, who was devoted to his brother, came up to the alp, and begged Klaus not to starve himself to death up there. Klaus replied that that was hardly likely since he had not perished already. Klaus had a secret motive for feeling so sure, but his answer hardly convinced his brother. Others, besides Peter, came up to see the one-time judge and councillor in his hideout among the briars and brambles, and these visitors, probably with very mixed intentions, gave him no peace. There was nothing for it now; Klaus was being stared at and overrun by curious neighbours. He had feared to be a laughing stock, had feared to be misunderstood by his neighbours, and now not even this was spared him. In the words of his own prayer: God had now taken him from himself, and it is precisely in this moment that he is given to God as wholly His. The apparent defeat and degradation is the last purification Klaus had to pass through in order to be completely God's, in order to be His perfect instrument. This is the supreme moment for Klaus: he has embraced the cross completely and has died to himself; within his own soul he is 'stripped and poor and naked'; it no longer matters to him what people think; grace has triumphed; everything that hinders him from being unreservedly God's has been surrendered; he has abandoned himself completely to divine providence. He has forsaken 'home and wife and children and fields for God's name' – what home and fields meant for Klaus perhaps only a farmer who has inherited the family farm, and in his turn will leave it, enriched with his labours, to his children, can fully appreciate. He has forsaken himself too now, and that is a very much greater thing. But no enumeration can give an adequate idea of his tremendous sacrifice.

The spell that had seemed to hang over the Ranft, preventing him from going there, is broken. Klaus is free now, free as he had not been while he was still bothered with fear and anxiety, and it is surely not fantasy to sense the freedom of his step as he leaves the Klisterli alp, crosses the hillside seeking another site, and then finally goes towards the Ranft. There suddenly he sees four lights coming down from heaven and indicating the spot God had chosen for him, the very site of the tower he had seen in his vision when he was sixteen. Klaus can doubt no longer. He has come home at last.

CHAPTER III

In the Ranft

At the end of what was, unhappily, the last of his articles on St Nicholas, Heinrich Federer wrote: 'The indulgent reader has perhaps followed me more or less willingly as far as the Ranft. Will he also dare to descend into the Ranft with me?' Rightly the poet saw a new chapter was starting in Klaus's life. He saw vividly the starkness of what was in front of Dorothea's husband: 'the watch, the fast, the agony of prayer'. And yet, surely, at this moment there must have been a sense of enormous relief. It is as though Klaus were climbing a mountain towards alpine pastures. For years, uncertain of his footsteps, he had been tentatively groping his way in the clouds, but now he has climbed above them. The way up to the summit will still be arduous, but however trying it may prove it will no longer be in the fog of uncertainty and bewilderment.

Neither eating nor drinking

The most striking element of the new chapter is Klaus's complete abstinence. Although the earliest sources do not explicitly refer to the incident under the hedge near Liestal as the beginning of his complete fast, it is usually considered to have started at that moment, so vividly described by the hermit himself. As we have seen, Klaus had already, for many years, restricted his food on four days in the week to the barest minimum: a small piece of bread or a few dried pears, but an absolute fast is something quite different, and Klaus realized that. Hans von Waldheim, who admittedly, has somewhat telescoped the incidents here, not mentioning the stay on the Klisterli alp, wrote that Klaus's fast dated from the moment he left Dorothea. If that is exact, then it was either while he was still on the alp or as soon as he arrived in the Ranft, that Klaus sent for his confessor, Oswald Yssner, who had been parish priest of Kerns since, at least, 1455. (For a short period, about 1462-3, he seems to have attended lectures at the newly-founded university of Basle.) It was probably Peter who fetched him, at Klaus's request. It says a lot for Yssner's zeal and for the respect he had for Klaus that he came at once.

The Parish Register contains Yssner's deposition on their meeting: 'At that time [this immediately follows the mention of the incident at Liestal], he began to abstain from natural food, and he persevered in this abstinence up till the eleventh day. Then Brother Klaus sent for him [Yssner] to ask his advice secretly whether he should eat or whether he should try to carry on, for it had ever been his longing to live without eating, so as to be more free from the world.'

Yssner proceeded most cautiously; he felt Klaus's bones, he examined him up and down, discovering how little flesh there was on him and that he was but skin and bone with his cheeks sunken and his lips cracked. It was clear to Yssner that Klaus was not deceiving him in saying that he had not eaten for eleven days. The next thing to be sure of was Klaus's motive in fasting, and once Yssner was sure it was out of love of God, he advised Klaus, since God had preserved him without any food for eleven days, to continue his fast, so far as he could do so without starving himself to death. The priest clearly did not want the whole thing to end in disaster, and it was only natural that he should insist Klaus stop were he to feel starvation approaching. Klaus continued, however, for the remaining nineteen and a half years of his life.

It was not long before the news that Klaus was neither eating nor drinking went the round of the neighbouring villages and hamlets. It is unlikely that Yssner had talked about it; the first to realize what was happening had been Peter, and now that Klaus had settled in the Ranft, his family and near neighbours will have noticed that he did not seem to be eating. Wölflin relates that with the help of neighbours he built a tiny log cabin in the Ranft. So near home, it seems only natural to wonder why it was neighbours and not his sons who helped him to build. This is perhaps significant, and probably casts further light on his reluctance to fix on the Ranft as the definitive site of his hermitage. These friends, so willing to help Klaus, probably wanted to bring him food and drink, or to share with him what they had brought for themselves. It was a blessing they had not much to do on their own farms during those November days and could help their friend, whose choice of way of life they seem to have approved. The slope on which they built the little cabin was much more wooded than it is now, and part of their work must have been clearing the site. The little hermitage was built on the hillside, not far from the bank of the Melchaa, which in this spot is a raging torrent.

Swiss were no more ready to believe in the extraordinary in the fifteenth century than they are today, and it is not surprising to find differences of opinion about Klaus's fast. There were some who at once believed in a miracle; some suspected members of the family of bringing him food secretly, while others quite simply said that Klaus was a fraud. He had made enemies, who would have been irked by a miraculous intervention for it would have told against them and put popular opinion on his side. It was probably only two years or so since he had withdrawn from local politics, and memories are not short in villages. The sceptics were people of such weight that finally at a meeting of the council Klaus and his fast were discussed. The outcome was the posting of guards to watch Klaus, and to make sure that nobody was bringing him provisions. Whether Klaus was aware of the watch is not known, but it is more than likely that Dorothea knew of it, and perhaps suffered from the suspicions of which her husband was the object. Klaus must have been followed and spied on as he went to Mass on Sunday, but he may not even then have noticed anything unusual being deep in prayer – there is a legend that he recited but one Our Father all the way from the Ranft to the parish church. After a month the guards were withdrawn – they had discovered nothing suspicious – and Klaus and his visitors were left unmolested.

From the beginning of his life as a hermit Klaus wore nothing but a long brown woollen tunic. He went barefoot and bareheaded. When he left his hermitage he carried a stick and a rosary. Two tunics, one preserved at Sachseln and one at Lucerne, help to picture Klaus as he then was, and serve to authenticate the two earliest representations of him: the small statue made of limewood, dating from 1504, now in the Town Hall at Stans, and the painting (1492), once on the high altar at Sachseln, and now again, after very many years when it seemed lost, in the church there. These succeed in presenting Klaus the hermit as no other later work of art does, yet they are strikingly different and portray, as it were, two moods of Klaus. A passage in the 'Pilgrim's Treatise': 'He stared at me with his mouth open' seems to suggest that the statue has fixed a characteristic attitude of Klaus. During the early period in the Ranft Klaus certainly continued to divide his day round the meditation of the

Das älteste Bild des Heiligen Bruder Klaus gemalt 1492, 5 Jahre nach seinem Tode (The earliest picture of Nicholas of Flüe, painted in 1492, five years after his death).

Passion of our Lord; he gave the whole morning to prayer and meditation, and in the afternoon, if it were fine, he went out, across the Melchaa and up into the woods.

Klaus had lived for nearly a year in the little log cabin he had built with his neighbours' help, when he once more figured on the district council's agenda. The council now acknowledged that he was no hypocrite, and that he was not moved by a spirit of fanaticism. They decided to build at public expense a chapel; they further decreed each man was to contribute his share of the work involved in building it. The chapel, on the spot where his little house had been erected, was to be dedicated in honour of the Virgin Mother of Christ. On to the rear of the chapel a tiny dwelling, approximately 10 feet long, 9 feet broad, and only 5 feet 11 inches high, was built in pinewood. There were tiny windows facing north and west, and a larger one, about 3 feet high, through which Klaus could look, unseen, onto the altar of the chapel. A lower floor or kind of cellar was built in which they placed, later on at least, a stove. The undertaking was a communal action; already the pride in their own 'living saint' is apparent among the country folk of Unterwalden. The tiny hermitage is still as it was then, so that it is possible to envisage Klaus there, but the chapel was rebuilt, after a landslide, at the end of the seventeenth century on the original groundplan.

To his summary description of the council's decision and its realization, Wölflin adds something which comes as a painful surprise. The decision and undertaking were opposed by Klaus's own kinsfolk, who declared that, before deciding upon such a laborious and expensive enterprise, it would be better to have greater proofs in favour of the hermit, and a longer period of perseverance in his way of life. How closely related to Klaus these 'kinsfolk' were is not known, or why,

Flüell Ranft.

when the council was openly in his favour, they continued to put difficulties in the way. The vagueness of the term perhaps intentionally hid the identity of a very close relative. Perhaps it was his eldest sons, fearful that things might go wrong and injure the family name, who were so reluctant to see public money and services devoted to Klaus.

Despite the opposition, the men of Unterwalden went on with their project, and when the chapel and hermitage were completed they unconditionally made them over to Klaus. All this coming and going to the chapel will have helped wonderfully in making a real path from the hamlet on the hilltop down to the hermitage. The visitors were increasing in number; Klaus was talked about, not only in Unterwalden but in the whole of the Confederation. His visitors were not only lay people but also priests. Heinrich am Grund early came to visit his friend, and talked to him about his fast. He was the first to whom Klaus spoke at length about the way he had come 'to this condition'. From Yssner he seems only, at first, to have sought advice on what to do, and to have discussed his abstinence with him only insofar as it was necessary for his confessor to be able to judge his motives.

It may have been in connection with the chapel that the Bishop of Constance first heard about Klaus. As has already been mentioned, the parish priest of Sachseln, Hans Burkard, does not appear at all in Klaus's life, and it may have been the parishioners who asked the bishop to consecrate the chapel. Wölflin says that the men of Unterwalden approached the authorities so that Klaus might have official approval, thereby protecting Unterwalden from the jealous suspicions of those who denied their claim to have such a divine gift in their district. The draft of his instructions to the auxiliary bishop, visiting the Swiss cantons in April, admirably illustrates the bishop's care for his flock. Hermann von Breitenlandenberg, who was Bishop of Constance from 1466 to 1474, did all in his power to bring peace into his diocese. This very year, 1469, he made a pact (an 'Eternal Peace') with the Confederates, hoping to make a more fruitful administration possible. The instructions he made out for Bishop Thomas Weldner speak with respect of the hermit, Nicholas, and imply that the reports the bishop had received were from reliable sources and quite favourable. He speaks of the good Klaus was doing, of the many people of both sexes who went to visit him in the belief that he was a saint and that by visiting him they would gain merit. But the bishop declared it was his duty to act to discover the truth, since the whole affair might be a fraud and if he did not intervene the simple faithful could be led astray, with danger to their souls. He then authorized the auxiliary to do everything possible to find out the truth of the matter, and promptly to inform him of the results of the investigation so that he might take the steps necessary to safeguard his people.

Bishop Thomas Weldner had plenty to do in the inner Swiss districts in the second half of April, 1469. On the second Sunday after Easter, 16 April, he consecrated the church of St Michael at Zug; then he rode the few miles to Oberwil, where, on the next day, he blessed the chapel. From Oberwil he went on into the neighbouring canton of Schwyz and blessed chapels at Oberarth and Goldau, and on 22 April reconciled the parish church of Muotatal. It was a lot for one week, but his journey took him on through the glorious Urner countryside to Altdorf, and then to Attinghausen, where on Monday the 24th he consecrated an altar in the church. As the eagle flies it is not a very great distance from this Urner village to the Ranft, but Bishop Thomas had a considerable roundabout route to follow, probably going in part by boat across the Lake of Lucerne. On Thursday, 27 April, he dedicated the Ranft hermitage chapel, and then spent a great part of the day with Klaus talking about sacred things. After various questions, the bishop asked the hermit what was the greatest virtue and the most pleasing to God. On Klaus answering that it was obedience, the bishop brought out bread and wine which he had with him, and, breaking the bread into three pieces, he commanded Klaus in virtue of holy obedience, to eat the bread. (Klaus saw obedience as the surest manifestation of charity, which is of course the greatest virtue.) Much put out by the command, Klaus begged the bishop to be satisfied if he ate only one of the pieces, broken into three. The bishop allowed this, but it was only with the greatest difficulty Klaus could take them, while he could hardly swallow the tiny amount of wine without vomiting. The bishop was upset at the pain caused to Klaus, but he was satisfied with the experiment. He assured Klaus that he had only tried him on the express instructions of the diocesan bishop, and not because he himself wanted to be difficult. Klaus knew that the bishop's request was not only a test of his obedience but also in the nature of a testing of the spirit animating him. It is not hard to believe the report that Klaus suffered terrible pains in the stomach for forty days after this incident.

Klaus's pleasure that the chapel had been consecrated can well be imagined. It was *his* chapel, and the choice of patrons gives a further glimpse into his world of prayer. The chapel was dedicated to Our Lady; the choice can cause no surprise for Klaus's great devotion to the Mother of God is known from other sources. The patronal feast was kept on the Assumption, 15 August. The secondary patronal feasts were the Exaltation of the Holy Cross, St Mary Magdalen, and the 10,000 Martyrs. Klaus's constant meditation on the

Passion of Our Lord prompted him to choose the feast of the Cross; Hans von Waldheim's diary reveals his devotion to St Mary Magdalen, but a word of explanation is needed for the last choice. These purely legendary soldier martyrs, now completely forgotten, enjoyed widespread popularity in the West after the Crusades; they were said to have been crucified for their faith on Mt. Ararat. A feast was kept in their honour on 22 June and the Swiss had a great devotion to them, doubtless owing to the military exploits, against overwhelming odds, related in their legend.

The happy outcome of Bishop Thomas Weldner's visit, and the gifts sent for the chapel and for the endowment by the Bishop of Constance, set the seal of ecclesiastical approval on Klaus's vocation, and probably served yet further to encourage visits to him. A couple of months after the bishop, a Dominican came to the Ranft; clearly Klaus was quickly at his ease for he gave his visitor much of his day, having various spiritual talks with him. It was the Octave day of Corpus Christi, 8 June. The next day they again talked together. The friar warned Klaus above all against vanity. To this Klaus replied that he was rarely moved to vanity. The Dominican then asked him how he had deserved the condition related of him, namely, living without eating, and whether it was true. Klaus replied that the question was a difficult one, and that he had explained himself only to one person (Heinrich am Grund), but that if the friar promised not to mention anything until after Klaus's death he would answer his questions. The sentences that do follow are so revealing that the abrupt breaking off in the narrative which comes so quickly is very disappointing.

Once Klaus had the advice of Yssner, his confessor, he does not seem to have thought about his fast any longer, but these first years in the Ranft had as a recurring theme the preoccupation with Klaus's fast of the civil and ecclesiastical authorities as well as of individuals. Briefly something must be said about it. First of all we are justified in inferring a miraculous intervention; natural causes can supply no explanation of the phenomenon, which is accepted as an historical fact by Catholics and Protestants alike. Secondly, using Herbert Thurston's words, it must be pointed out that 'the existence of heroic sanctity is not guaranteed by any charismata however remarkable, but only by a consistently virtuous conduct in the trials of daily life and by an adequate use of the opportunities which may present themselves of promoting the service and glory of God.' In other words, Klaus's holiness is independent of the gift of total abstinence. Finally, however, despite the foregoing remarks, the fast did have a role in Klaus's special vocation, for it was on account of it that many of his compatriots looked on him as a saint, and so heeded his advice on personal and public matters. In a letter to the Duke of Milan, Bernardino Imperiali said that he visited the hermit, 'who is considered a saint, because he does not eat'. The Milanese Ambassador simply states here the current opinion without comment, but his words are a valuable testimony to what was thought among the Swiss. This attribution of not eating, as a primary factor in Brother Klaus's reputation for holiness, was repeated some fifty years later in the instance of Elizabeth Barton, The Holy Maid of Kent 1506-34. (cf. Alan Neame's valuable study of this much maligned young woman, p.82.)

Visitors

Klaus's fame spread quickly across the frontiers of the confederation, and many visitors came to him. Curiosity to see the hermit, who neither ate nor drank, was almost inevitably mingled in a greater or lesser degree with higher motives. In contemporary letters and sermons these visits are mentioned, and the impression Klaus made is described. Among those who visited the Ranft were well-known figures like Geiler of Kaisersberg, who came in 1471 or 1472 while he was still lecturing at the University of Basle; like the Dominican Felix Fabri, whose father and uncle (Burgermeister Stüssi) had been killed by the Confederates at S. Jakob an der Sihl – his visit is all the more remarkable since he had a lifelong antipathy towards the Swiss; as had Peter Schott and his father from Strassburg, who probably came in the summer of 1482. Klaus had made up his mind 'to seek out some place in solitude, fit only for contemplation' but from quite early in his eremitical life there were outside contacts. The visitors who wrote about their visits had been originally moved mainly by curiosity, but there were many who came for advice and help from someone close to God. They did not invade Klaus's solitude, his being alone with God: he came to them from there. This is not unusual: Julian of Norwich, Seraphium of Sarov and, in our own day, Thomas Merton are typical. Interestingly both von Waldheim and von Bonsterten mention that Klaus went away from his cell for greater solitude for three hours each day and sometimes for a day or two.

One of the earliest visitors, Ulrich, was a Swabian, who sought out Klaus, because he was thoroughly disillusioned with life (or perhaps with what he had made of it!). Received in a friendly fashion he was encouraged to tell Klaus that he had come to find a refuge for his life, and salvation for his soul. He did not intend to content himself with one fleeting visit, but wanted to become a hermit not far from Klaus, promising he would observe all the hardships of a hermit's life. Klaus pointed out a spot on the other side of the Melchaa, suitable for a hermitage – it was probably on land belonging to the von Flües – and there he built himself a tiny house. Ulrich, a small, plump, rather talkative individual, was already getting on in years when he settled in the Ranft, and it was Klaus who did the visiting, crossing the river and going up to talk to his fellow hermit, when he believed it was necessary. Visitors to Klaus often crossed to visit Ulrich, or sought him out when Klaus was not to be found. He was literate and had books in his cell, but he was reticent about his past. The innkeeper at Kerns told Hans von Waldheim, who had been put out by Ulrich's evasive answers, that this Swabian nobleman had been a brigand before his conversion, but perhaps this was only the local people's gossip. At first Ulrich had only his little house, with a kind of porch but later he too had a chapel. He outlived Klaus, and died at an advanced age on 2 June 1491, and was buried in the churchyard at Kerns, to which parish that side of the river belongs. His chapel still stands on the other side of the Melchaa, visible from Flüeli.

Perhaps the most pathetic of all Klaus's known visitors was Heinrich von Hunwil. Although it would be an exaggeration to say he had played a leading role in Swiss politics, he certainly had been influential beyond his own canton. He had been only twenty-six when first elected chief magistrate (*Schultheiss*), the leading governmental position in Lucerne. It was he who, in his official capacity, had presented Heinrich am Grund, in 1465, to the bishop for appointment as parish priest of Kriens. Towards the end of 1473 he was accused of dishonest machinations; although the Council in October declared him blameless, and elected him for a twelfth turn of office in December, he was terribly upset. A kind of persecution mania took hold of him; he began to accuse himself of crimes against the state and to believe everyone was against him. It was in January of 1474 that he wended his way to the hermitage beside the Melchaa, and there he poured out his tale of woe to Klaus, asking his advice and begging his prayers. Klaus had a remarkable gift for consoling the sad and dejected, but this time things did not improve, and when von Hunwil died in August that year, rumour had it he had taken his own life. Like Dostoevsky's staretz, Klaus with his deep sympathy for the sufferer will hardly have hesitated to pray for him.

Two visits to Klaus, described at some length, are well worth quoting, providing as they do a picture of life in the Ranft. The first of these was made in 1474 by a rich nobleman of Halle in Saxony, Hans von Waldheim. In the spring of that year he had gone on a pilgrimage to the sanctuaries in the South of France, and had kept a diary recording all he saw and heard that interested him. On his way home he put up at 'The Bell' in Bern, and here, on the feast of the Ascension, he met the prior of Eisenach, a Charterhouse in Saxe-Weimar. The Carthusian had just come from a visit to the Ranft, and told the Saxon all about it. Hans von Waldheim had heard about Klaus from a merchant at the annual fair at Halle, the previous year, and had made a note in his diary that should he ever come into Klaus's country he would enquire about him, so he decided now to make a slight detour to visit Klaus. He stabled his horses at Lucerne, and on Wednesday, 25 May, he hired a boat to take him and his valet across the lake to Rotzloch. Accompanied by the boatmen he arrived towards evening at Kerns, where he put up at the inn. The landlord guessed his destination, and, pointing out that access to Klaus was not at all easy, proposed they enlisted the aid of the local parish priest, confessor to the hermit. Oswald Yssper was invited to supper, and during the meal promised to accompany von Waldheim on the following day to the Ranft.

The innkeeper let von Waldheim have one of his best horses, and early in the morning of Thursday, 26 May, the little party set off. (How many visitors to Switzerland since then have had the same experience as von Waldheim who noted: 'We journeyed half a mile; in our country it would have been called a good mile!') En route, hearing that von Waldheim was keen on seeing Klaus's wife and son, the priest detailed off the boatboy to tell Dorothea that he was going to offer Mass, and that if she wished to assist, she was to come, bringing her youngest son with her.

'We went on,' wrote von Waldheim, 'and reached Brother Klaus's hermitage. The Swiss have built on to the hermitage a chapel with three altars. In the chapel the priest asked me what Mass I would like. I chose that of St. Mary Magdalen. Whereupon he went to the altar and looked for it; when he had found it, he turned round and noticed Brother Klaus's wife with her son. He introduced me to them. I shook hands with her and her son, and wished them "Good morning". She is still young and pretty, not yet forty; she has a pleasant unwrinkled face. I asked: "Dear lady, how long is it now since Brother Klaus left you?" She said: "This lad, my son, will be seven on St. John the Baptist's Day. When the boy was thirteen weeks old, that is on St. Gall's Day, Brother Klaus left me and since then has never come back to me." I chatted like that for quite a while with the woman and her son; the youngster carries himself well, like Brother Klaus, and is as like him as can be; I gave him some money...

'Brother Klaus is a slim man, about my age, in the prime of life, in his fifties. He has brown hair, without a single grey one. His thin distinguished face has a good colour; he is a tall upright man, and speaks a pleasant German... It is his custom, when he wants to give himself to contemplation, to go into the forest alone for a day or two. It is said that he has often been seen at Our Lady of Einsiedeln but that no one has ever met him en route. How or by what paths he gets there is surely known to God alone.

'Before I came to Brother Klaus, I had been told that his body lacked natural warmth, that his hands were cold as ice, that his face was yellower and paler than that of a dead man about to be buried. Further that he was always sad and never happy. I must say, however, that I did not find in him a single one of these characteristics. First of all he had a normal temperature; his hands were as warm as those of anybody else. My valet, Kunz, and I took hold of them four or five times. His face was neither yellow nor pale, but of a normal colour, like any healthy person. He was not sad, but in all he had to say and to do we found him affable, communicative, sociable and friendly about everything.'

Another visitor's words about his farewell from Klaus back up this description. The pilgrim, whose treatise will be mentioned later and who probably frequently visited the hermit during his early years in the Ranft, wrote: 'He took me in his arms, embracing me, and said God grant you salvation and good fortune.'

'But,' von Waldheim wrote, 'to come back to my narrative. The parish priest of Kerns offered God and us the Mass of St. Mary Magdalen in Brother Klaus's chapel. When the Mass was over, he went and asked admittance for me, and led me and my valet to Brother Klaus's cell which adjoins the chapel. As we entered the hermitage, Brother Klaus received us with a happy, smiling face and shook hands with us; his hands were not cold but naturally warm. He begged us to wait a moment while he spoke to the people who had assisted at the Mass. Thereupon he opened the window and said: "God grant you a good and blessed morning, dear friends and people." They thanked him. Then he shut the window and sat down with us. I told him that I had come from distant lands to St. Mary Magdalen, to St. Anne, to St. Anthony and to other saints and also to him. Hearing that he said: "I had my chapel dedicated to St. Mary Magdalen." So I told him the legends of St. Mary Magdalen . . . and I told him so much that his eyes filled with tears. After that he talked to us about heavenly things. I asked him then: "Dear Brother Klaus, I have heard it said, both at home and here, that you neither eat nor drink, and that this has been so for several years. Is that so?" He replied: "God knows." '

Von Waldheim then noted down Brother Klaus's account of the interview with the bishop, at the end of which he again put his question:

'And have you not eaten or drunk since then?' But I got nothing more out of him than 'God knows.' After much further conversation I took leave of him and recommended myself to his fervent prayers. He shook hands with us and so we departed. It so happened, as we went away, it came to me there was something further I had wanted to speak to him about, so I asked the priest to arrange for me to see him again. That was done; we went again to him and he received us with outstretched hands. I told him what I had in mind, and then once more shaking hands we left him. While we were still in front of the chapel, Brother Klaus came out and called the priest, who is his confessor, to him, and spoke softly to him. Then we left.

A visitor who came in 1477 stayed for a whole year. This was the parish priest of Horw, who had obtained leave of absence to do so. All that is known of him for certain is that he was a close friend of Heinrich am Grund, probably Johann Schnider by name. But his presence in the Ranft must have been particularly welcome to Brother Klaus for it meant in all likelihood frequent Mass.

On 31 December, 1478, Brother Klaus received a visit from Albert von Bonstetten, Dean of Einsiedeln, who later described his visit in letters to several leading religious and political personages. The description contrasts sharply with von Waldheim's, not only in its style but also, to some extent, in its contents. The effect on Brother Klaus of a vivid vision has been surmised to have made the difference in the impressions he made on von Waldheim and von Bonstetten, but it was more likely due to the different times of the year and even more to the visitors themselves.

After Mass, celebrated by a priest who accompanied them, von Bonstetten and his party were received by Brother Klaus, through the intermediary of the *Landamman*.

> The servant of God awaited us in the upper part of the hermitage. As he saw us, he said, softly and humbly, but in a manly voice, and holding himself erect and uncovered: 'Be greeted in God's Name, very dear Fathers and Brothers,' and thereupon he shook hands with us in the correct order. Quite stupefied we all thanked him. As for myself, my hair stood on end and my tongue clove to my cheek. 'Why ever have you come to this wild gorge at the world's end? To see me, a poor sinner? I fear you will not find in me anything worthy of such gentlemen.' 'Yes, everything,' we replied with one voice, 'everything that is pleasing to God and fitting in a soldier of Jesus Christ and a servant of God.' 'Would to God that it were so,' he replied, and then: 'Come down into the warm.'

Von Bonstetten said that Brother Klaus's answers to their questions were those of an illiterate person, but were, nevertheless, well chosen and supernatural, so that not even someone ill disposed towards him could have taken exception.

He describes the hermit:

He is of a good height, very thin, brown and wrinkled, his hair is not thick, but is in disorder and uncombed, it is black going grey. His beard is a couple of inches long; his eyes are ordinary, the whites clear; his teeth are sparklingly white and regular; his nose is in harmony with the rest of his face. He is not talkative, and does not address those whom he does not know. I would say he is about sixty. If you touch him his hand is cold. He is bareheaded and barefooted; all that he has on is a grey tunic. On this St. Sylvester's Day the little room was hardly warm . . . I saw no crockery, nor table, nor blanket on which the servant of God could rest. He must stand or sit, or stretch out on the floor in the dust if he wants to lie down.

Bonstetten then describes the visit Brother Klaus had encouraged them to make to Ulrich. Before closing his letter he added to his eyewitness account of Brother Klaus what he had heard from reliable sources:

They say that he sleeps half standing, leaning against the wall. At the beginning of his eremitical life he was troubled by the evil spirit, who buffeted him so much that several times visitors found him half dead on the floor. Every day, and particularly in summer, he leaves his cell for about three hours, going to pray in a cave. He praises highly obedience and peace; with much insistence he urges the Confederates and all who come to him to keep peace.

Not all his clerical visitors were as peaceable as this party, nor was the hermit always so mild with them. In 1482 a visiting priest was very troublesome, seeking to trap Brother Klaus with questions about the Blessed Trinity, and the doctrine and discipline of the Church. Failing to find anything wrong in his answers, the priest threatened to send someone even more qualified to examine him. When the Obwalden authorities got to know about this visitor, they were so concerned, perhaps suspecting he had something to

Porträt v. Hl. Bruder Klaus, ca.1504.
(Statue of Nicholas of Flüe, c. 1504.)

do with the Inquisition, that they wrote to the government of Lucerne, asking them to examine the credentials of people who said they were on their way to the Ranft.

Three years later, in October 1485, Abbot Conrad of Wiblingen and Abbot George of St Stephen's in Wurzburg visited Brother Klaus, while they were making a canonical visitation of the Benedictine monasteries of the diocese of Constance. Their visit is recorded in the annals of Hirsau, but, discreetly, Abbot George is not named; the annalist mentions however that he heard about the incident from Abbot Conrad. Their detour to the Ranft was due chiefly to the Abbot of Wurzburg's curiosity. The annals say that though Abbot George was a little bit too keen on the riches of this world, thrifty and avaricious, he was a devout and learned man! He seems not to have been in a very good mood on arrival for at once he started to set traps for Brother Klaus, questioning him on various disputed scriptural problems, although he knew the hermit could not read. Brother Klaus, quietly and humbly and giving no sign of impatience, answered his questions unhesitatingly. After many other questions the 'abbatial tempter' said: 'So you are the man who boasts that he has not eaten for many years.' The hermit replied: 'My good father, I have never said, and do not say now, that I do not eat.' Still dissatisfied the abbot went on doing his best to trap his gentle host; the conversation turned on covetousness and Abbot George asked: 'What is avarice?' It was the last straw – the time for politeness was past, and the abbot, dumbfounded by the sudden change in the tall, peaceable, now furiously indignant man opposite him, got more than he bargained for:

Why do you question me, an illiterate penniless fellow, about avarice, when you being both learned and rich, not only know better than I what it is, but have even experienced yourself what goes on in the heart of an avaricious man? The year before last you bought twenty-seven measures of the best wine for a song, and then last year you passed it on again with a considerable profit. But your bishop upset your covetousness and punished it by his own cupidity; he took from you, and the buyer, all the twenty-seven measures of wine and put them into his own cellar. He has not paid you nor will he pay you a penny for them. The signs of your avarice are written on your forehead, they have taken root in your heart, and to your horror they are visible to others.

The annalist insists that although the transaction seems to have become common gossip in Benedictine monasteries, it was not known to Brother Klaus in that way, but through a revelation of the Holy Spirit. The intricacies of the deal that went so badly astray are recorded: the abbot had bought at the vintage twenty-seven measures of wine at six Rhenish gulden per measure. In the following year the price of wine went up and the abbot sold this reserve to a citizen of Nurnberg at twenty-four gulden per measure. The bishop heard about it, and, listening to malicious advisers, confiscated the wine before the buyer had his cart ready, loaded it on to a ship and brought it to his own cellar. All this was possible since the wine had not been brought to the monastery, but had been left in the village where the abbot had bought it.

Abbot Johannes Trithemius, the Hirsau annalist of the above incident, set Brother Klaus's example of fasting and abstinence before his monks at Spanheim in a sermon, about 1486. One passage seems to imply that he had actually visited the Ranft, with a theologian to whom his learning meant but little, and that he had heard Brother Klaus speak most eloquently about the sacrament of the altar to this professional.

78

Here and there in these visitors' reports some remarkable things stand out; some of them, like his infused knowledge of the scriptures and theology, or of the visiting abbot's fault, seem to be exterior aspects of his holiness; others, like his knowledge of the exact order of precedence among von Bonstetten's party, may be simply due to the presence of what psychologists call the psi faculty. Much more interesting, however, are the confidences he made to close friends, because they provide a glimpse of his inner life.

Confidences made to Friends

When Brother Klaus settled in the Ranft he was fifty years old, he had lived for more than twenty years with an attractive woman who had borne him ten children, and he was but a short distance from the home he had built for himself and his wife and family. There is no doubt he had experienced the genuine joys of married life. It was then to be expected that, like so many of the desert fathers who had become hermits only after living among the legitimate pleasures of the world – men to whom he has been compared – Brother Klaus would have been strongly tempted to long for what he had abandoned. If we realize that even the countryside was rich in memories of his married life, we shall see yet more clearly why he himself had expected to be troubled in this way. But in actual fact he was quite free of this trial, having neither desire nor longing nor temptation to return. He was gratefully conscious that this was a favour of God, and counted it among the three important graces which he particularly mentioned more than once to his friend, an der Halden, when they talked together. The other two graces were that he had obtained the consent of his wife and children to become a hermit, and that he was enabled to live without eating or drinking. When an der Halden recorded this last grace he thought it well to say that he believed Brother Klaus had not taken any natural food or drink during all the years he lived as a hermit.

Although Brother Klaus had no desire to return to his wife and family, the devil did make an effort to get him to change his mind. One day, the devil, in the form of a nobleman very richly dressed and splendidly mounted, Oswald Yssner says, came to Brother Klaus. He spoke for a long time with the hermit, and finally told him that he should abandon his eremitical life and do as other people, for he could not merit eternal life if he continued as he was. This attack was much subtler than those which he had had to suffer at the very beginning of his time in the Ranft, when the devil attacked him violently, but this too was overcome with the grace of Almighty God and the assistance of the immaculate Mother of God.

The following are without doubt the most amazing of the confidences made to friends and later recorded by them. The Sachseln Parish Register, after giving the testimony of an der Halden and Rorer, has that of his priest friends.

Heinrich am Grund, parish priest of Stans, related that Brother Klaus told him, that while he was in his mother's womb, before he was born, he saw in the heavens a star, which shone in the whole world, and ever since he had dwelt in the Ranft he had always seen a star in the heavens, which seemed to be the same (and that he was of opinion that it was he himself; this meant, as he explained, that everyone knew of him, that he thus shone in the world). Further Brother Klaus told him, that before his birth, in his mother's womb, he saw a great rock (this indicated the firmness and constancy of his life, in which he was to persevere and not fall away from his intentions). Also in his mother's womb he saw the holy oils.

And when he was born and came into the world, he recognized his mother and the midwife, and he saw himself carried to be baptised through the Ranft to Kerns, so consciously that he had never forgotten it, and what happened then was as vivid to him as if it had just happened. He saw then too, assisting at the baptism, an old man, whom he did not recognize.

Some recent biographers attribute the explanations (the passages in brackets) to am Grund. Wölflin, however, in the biography written while Brother Klaus's friends were still alive, attributed them quite simply to the hermit, adding that they were made without boasting.

It is difficult to know what to make of these statements. Two 'surprising mystics' of the last century, Anna Katharina Emmerich and Dominica Klara Moes, claimed that at the time of their baptism, shortly after their birth, they were alive to all the supernatural implications of the sacrament. Brother Klaus's claim does not go as far as this, and yet it too strains our credulity very near to breaking point. One is sorely tempted to dismiss it as unwitting self-deception, fruit of Brother Klaus's vivid realization of God's choice of him for a mission. A recent study by M-L. von Franz presents another hypothesis: Brother Klaus dreamt of these prenatal visions and the events at the christening, and he was so convinced of the truth of the dream that he considered its contents as genuine information. It is difficult, however, to be fully satisfied with such solutions, or with one which attributes the amazing claim to a misunderstanding by Heinrich am Grund (after all a learned man who knew Klaus intimately) of what the hermit told him.

A parallel that does appear valid is the joyful pre-natal recognition by St John the Baptist of the arrival at his parents' home of Christ in Mary's womb. It must be admitted moreover that remarkable things of a similar nature have been recorded of more recent historical personages, e.g. that Mozart from his third year 'used to amuse himself for hours trying out thirds on the harpsichord', that he composed at five, and wrote his first symphony at eight, or, to mention contemporaries, that the late Lt. Col. Oreste Pinto, of 'Spycatcher' fame, remembered things from his sixth month, and Sir Compton Mackenzie from his seventh. We are so much in the realm of the supernatural and of the extraordinary here in the Ranft with Brother Klaus that, bearing in mind also how little we really know of the powers of the soul, we shall not be far wrong if we accept what he said at its face value and appreciate it, above all, as God's way of making him aware of the demands one day to be made of him, and of the responsibility to accompany the graces so richly bestowed on him. (cf. the Appendix, p. 125.)

Two tantalizingly short passages, one in Eichorn the other in Wölflin, reveal another aspect of Brother Klaus's prayer. Eichorn recorded that Klaus was once found in ecstasy by some of his family. He was standing with his back against the wall, his eyes turned upward and strangely fixed, his mouth open, and his appearance somewhat terrifying. When he came to he said: 'Children, I've been in the village.' Eichorn insisted that this strange sentence only meant that Brother Klaus had been in spirit to visit his friends. But surely not even Eichorn himself can have been satisfied with this; it is more than likely that Klaus had used a colloquialism not understood by Eichorn. The expression seems probably to describe a joyful exhilarating experience. Durrer, suggesting it, illustrates the simple frankness of Klaus's language, sets it beside the expression Klaus used to a young visitor to indicate how easy and pleasant prayer might sometimes be: 'as if one were going dancing'. The two phrases were, interestingly enough, left in the original German though in each case the rest of the context was in Latin. These lines of Eichorn seem to indicate how perfectly the statue of 1504 has portrayed Klaus.

The passage of Wölflin is as follows: 'All those who came to him were, on first seeing him, quite bewildered. He said that the cause of this terror was that he had seen a human face, shining so vividly that at the sight of it he had become very much frightened, and his heart had as it were burst asunder into tiny pieces; quite terrified he had turned his face away and fallen prostrate to the ground; he said that it was because of this that his countenance appeared terrible to others.' Wölflin exaggerated in saying that all who approached Brother Klaus were frightened, for Bonstetten is the only visitor to mention the frightened reaction he and his companions experienced, and even in their case it is not clear that it was the hermit's appearance that disturbed them. The incident can, however, certainly be accepted as historical; unfortunately Wölflin said nothing about its meaning.

This vision would seem to have been an 'active presentation of God to the soul, with its psychological correlative an immediate intuition of God' and the fear it struck into Brother Klaus's heart is not surprising. Nicholas's experience can be described as a real vision of God's majesty, insofar as the inner eye of earthbound man is capable of perceiving and taking in the divine. St John's reaction at the first vision related in the Apocalypse (I,17) is somewhat similar: 'At the sight of him, I fell down at his feet like a dead man.' Perhaps, however, the reaction of the apostles at the Transfiguration of Our Lord will best help to understand what happened in the Ranft. In his constant meditation and prayer, centred round the Passion, Brother

Klaus, like the apostles, had grown in intimacy with Christ, had come to love and to attempt to imitate all the exquisite virtues and human qualities of his beloved Lord. Now, as the apostles on Mount Thabor, he is accorded a glimpse of the godhead, and, like them, (Mark IX,15) he was 'overcome with fear'. Brother Klaus knew, from an earlier vision, that those whose hearts were eaten up by self-love could not bear to look upon Christ because of their own sins, but this vision searingly impressed on him that even for those who love him there is an aspect of God which is awe-inspiring. A few lines from Maisie Spens may help: 'We have – and can have – no idea of the Reality and Power of Glory until God sends it as lightning to smite us to the ground like Peter, James and John. So swift the lightning of His glory when He chooses to send it, that neither physical nor spiritual eye, nor brain discern what is seen nor how. Only the subsequent *bouleversement* – and in it His making all things new - witnesses to the seeing that caused it.' The fear Brother Klaus experienced is the normal reaction of a human in vivid contact with the divine, and in his case it was so strong that, for a time at least, it was visible in his face.

A relic, preserved at Sarnen, is a silent witness to another aspect of Brother Klaus's inner life; a discipline made of black goat's hair, under an inch wide, about three feet long, and with an iron buckle at one end, which Gundelfingen mentions was found in his cell after his death. Fully to understand self-inflicted penance the saint's own vision is needed. We know St Paul wrote: 'I buffet my own body and make it my slave or I, who have preached to others, may myself be rejected as worthless,' and 'I am glad of my sufferings on your behalf, as, in this mortal frame of mine, I help to pay off the debt which the afflictions of Christ leave still to be paid, for the sake of His body the Church.' Yet, for us moderns, disciplines and hair shirts usually seem repugnant, perhaps because so few of us have the vision of a saint. It is perhaps, too, inevitable that in an age of overemphasis on material well-being, even Christians should be tempted to find the mortifications practised by saints an overemphasis on the spiritual, a contempt of the body, or even a denial of the fundamental unity of man. It is not known what impelled Brother Klaus to make use of this discipline; with his consciousness of a mission it may perhaps be supposed that he saw himself responsible for his fellow men, and because he loved them too much to want them to be punished for their sins, he punished himself, uniting his sufferings to those of Christ on the Cross.

As has already been mentioned Brother Klaus told his Dominican visitor of his 'great reverence and devotion towards the venerable sacrament of the body and blood of Jesus Christ'. To at least two others the hermit spoke of what the sacrifice of the Mass and Holy Communion meant to him. As the years went by and his penitent still did not eat anything, Oswald Yssner became more and more insistent he be given an explanation of this remarkable grace. One day, very secretly, in his hermitage, Brother Klaus told his confessor that 'when he assisted at Mass and the priest partook of the sacrament, he received such sustenance from it that he was enabled to live without eating or drinking, but that otherwise he could not do so.' The sentence is interesting: Klaus does not say that he was never hungry or thirsty, and more must not be read into his words than they contain. Further, Brother Klaus did not 'explain' his fast by his own monthly communions; it was the priest's communion that made it possible. In the fifteenth century when frequent communion, as it is known today, was not customary, devout Christians made much of their spiritual communions, and Yssner clearly understood when Brother Klaus referred to the spiritual communion he made at the moment the priest received the sacrament.

The second testimony is in the so-called 'Pilgrim's Treatise'. This work is thought to have been written by Ulrich Holler of Nurnberg, who is probably the first Ulrich mentioned by Wölflin, the intimate friend of Brother Klaus who settled in the Ranft during the last year of the hermit's life. There is something both lovable and naive about this German, whose attempt to imitate Klaus's fast was finally ended by a good meal prepared by Dorothea, and it is hardly surprising the treatise contains so much of Ulrich and so little of Brother Klaus. But that little is precious. The reference to the Holy Eucharist comes in the hermit's answer to the pilgrim's query on the nature of the bread asked for in the petition of the Lord's Prayer: 'Give us this day our daily bread.' The first sentence – in absolute accord with the greatest spiritual teachers of the Church – reveals Brother Klaus's penetrating vision of God's provident love; 'In all food the grace of almighty God is hidden, and is received; without it man could no more obtain nourishment than if he ate stones. In a hidden manner God goes in with His omnipotence into a tiny host, and it is then changed so that it is no longer natural bread, but only, invisibly, the flesh and blood with the ineffable goodness of the true God and Man. And in every host, consecrated by the priest, there remains perfectly, and in every particle, his undivided godhead.' The eloquent fervour of Brother Klaus seems to have remained in the pilgrim's memory as witness of what Holy Communion meant to him.

The 'pilgrim' noted other answers. One indicated Brother Klaus's devotion to the Blessed Virgin Mary, and his defence of the then still controverted doctrine of her immaculate

conception; another revealed his confidence in divine
providence and his awareness of the absolute need to remain
'in the truth': 'All will be well for the man who does not
depart from the truth and perseveres in the love of God.'
This sentence contains a deep psychological understanding
of human nature and a teaching that can never be stressed
enough; experience teaches how very often a crisis, a period
when 'all is not well', springs in great part from a 'departing
from the truth' – a departing which may not even be fully
conscious. Biographically the following passage is invaluable:
'And he (Brother Klaus) continued: "If it does not bore you
I would like to show you my book. In it I read and seek to
penetrate this doctrine [he had just spoken of the Holy
Eucharist]." And he brought me a design resembling a wheel
with six spokes as it is represented here.'

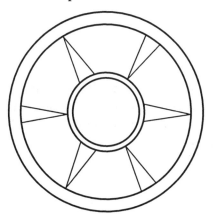

The pilgrim relates how Brother Klaus then proceeded to
explain to him the meaning of this wheel with its six spokes,
of which three came to a point at the hub, and the other
three at the rim. The former three represented the three
divine persons, who proceed from the one godhead and
embrace Heaven and all the earth in their power. Of the

other three spokes one symbolized God's entering into and proceeding from the womb of the maiden Mary without violating her virginity; another the immensity of Almighty God in the tiny host, given to us as our food, and which is the human body He took at the Incarnation together with His indivisible godhead; and the third represented our life which is but short and passing, and yet long enough for us to merit, by the love of God, an ineffable happiness which will know no end.

These passages from the 'Pilgrim's Treatise' make Brother Klaus come alive; they reveal his thought and prayer far more than the developments in the second part of the treatise which can be left aside without much loss. In the passage on his 'book' the hermit is seen making use of something familiar to him as a farmer, transforming the wheel into a tiny manual of theology, and even more into a vehicle for his speculation. The wheel in its simplicity is far more revealing than the complicated development of the picture preserved in the church at Sachseln. The 'developed' picture, even admitting it dates from the last years of Brother Klaus seems to be the fruit of suggestions made rather by the pilgrim than by the hermit. Only those who have themselves made use of such symbols can fully appreciate Brother Klaus's wheel, and will be far from calling it naive. His need to think for himself, the intellectual side of his make-up, stands out quite vividly in these lines. It is wrong to labour the 'illiterate peasant' motive, instead the very necessity Klaus had of thinking for himself needs stressing; for Klaus, as for any Christian with a deep faith in divine things as well as the capacity and need for thinking, thinking about the object of his faith became a 'must'. He was eager to go on learning more about the main doctrines of Christianity by constant, prayerful pondering on them, and also, at least in two or three of the answers, it is clear he was not unwilling to instruct others (layman though he was) and to do so with firmness, even in the then disputed matter of the immaculate conception of the Blessed Virgin Mary. There is a happy legend which says that Mary rewarded Klaus's devotion to her by appearing to him on an apple tree close to the Melchaa, where today the lower Ranft chapel stands.

One last witness must be called before we turn from this study of Brother Klaus's adoration and contemplation of the divine mysteries, which enabled him to give advice and help and become a spiritual father to so many of his visitors. In 1479 there came to the hermit in the Ranft a 'great and very learned doctor' of theology, who put seven questions to Brother Klaus. Since the questions come from the theologian the answers give hardly as spontaneous an expression of the hermit's spiritual preoccupations as his words to the pilgrim, yet they are very indicative. To the question what was the noblest and the best that God had given to man, Brother Klaus replied: 'That is the reason and the soul.' Asked whence the soul came he said: 'From God's fatherly heart.' The third question was: 'What is the greatest thing we can give God?' and Brother Klaus answered: 'That which he has given us.' The learned doctor then asked in what way we can in all humility repay him, and the answer was: 'By keeping God's commandments.' The fifth question was what was the greatest of these commandments, and the answer was: 'The love of God.' Asked whether he doubted if God would punish sins, he replied: 'I do not doubt that God will punish sins, here or beyond.' Finally he was asked whether he did not believe that God was capable of forgiving a man who had been responsible for all the sins in the world, and he answered: 'If the man comes to sorrow and to confession, and sins no more, God is certainly able to forgive him.'

CHAPTER IV

Pater Patriae

The Swiss call St Nicholas of Flüe the Father of their country, a title due above all to his intervention at the Diet of Stans in December 1481. Adequately to appreciate his action there demands more than a knowledge of the course of events at the diet: the background of that scene must be sketched in outline, although, in effect, that background is one aspect of a whole century of Swiss history.

Background to the Diet of Stans

The signatories of the Covenant of Sempach in 1393 were equally representative of town and country: four towns and four country districts. During most of the fifteenth century the country districts strove vigorously to maintain this representative equality although it was hardly in accord with reality. They were suspicious of the towns, often without justification, and the hostility, which had been present in the fourteenth century, grew alarmingly all through the fifteenth, accentuated and aggravated by several causes. Motives of economy and strategy were primarily responsible for Switzerland's expansion, but even this expansion added fuel to the flames of jealousy and hostility, and the interior development of the Confederation was paralysed by dissensions, springing in great part from the opposition between town and country.

Criminal as this opposition appears now, it was viewed as such, in those centuries, by only a few far-sighted figures of whom St Nicholas of Flüe is the greatest. The country districts, ravaged more than once during the wars, resented the apparent prosperity of the towns and their political development along aristocratic lines; they believed themselves faithful to the spirit of the origins of the Confederation and clung to popular government. Their impoverishment due to the military campaigns had led to agrarian disturbances and to emigration, which had taken the form of mercenary service in foreign armies. But the country districts were not alone in feeling the effects of the wars; Zurich had been ruined by the long civil conflict which had lasted, with interruptions, from 1439 to 1446, and which some historians consider as primarily responsible for the demoralization during the last quarter of the fifteenth century. The most serious symptoms of the malaise in Switzerland were the bribery and corruption in public life, and abuse of revenues and pensions obtained from foreign rulers, and the extensive enlisting in foreign armies.

This foreign mercenary service must be properly understood if it is not to be condemned outright. It was to earn a livelihood these men left home, and since they were renowned as soldiers, they were willingly accepted as such by foreign powers. There was no question for them of devotion to a cause, so that their service was simply a profession like any other; but there was hardly a profession that could have been more demoralizing. The soldiers who returned home with their pay and their arms found their families poor and discontented. Love of war (because it was their profession) and love of money led to corruption among the leaders and to a spirit of indiscipline and anarchy among the rank and file. From this sprang a long line of civil disturbances, of which the one nearest to Brother Klaus was the revolt of the Entlebuch in 1478; this was a wretched affair in which Obwalden had schemed to detach the Entlebuch from Lucerne by an uprising of the peasantry. A more serious disturbance, a direct consequence of the Burgundian war, occurred in 1477. It seems to have started as a 'huge joke' perpetrated by a group of 'angry young men' during the carnival, but developed into a plundering expedition, terrorizing parts of Switzerland, from the Lake of Lucerne to the Lake of Geneva; it was directed against the towns in general, and against Geneva in particular, since this city was in the Confederates' debt – it had been spared by them during the war, at a price not yet paid!

Since Brother Klaus was concerned less with the Burgundian war than with its consequences, it will suffice to summarize briefly the war and the events leading up to it. Charles the Bold, Duke of Burgundy (1465-1477), had gradually extended his territory and was fast becoming the most powerful monarch in Europe, when the collision with the Swiss, which, viewed at a distance of five centuries, seems to have been inevitable, came in 1474. In the spring of that year the Confederates had concluded an 'eternal peace' with Austria (it was during the preparations for this treaty that Duke Sigismund approached Brother Klaus with the gift of a chalice, probably through his physician, Burkhard von Horneck, who came to visit the hermit). This peace treaty was part of the French diplomatic manoeuvre to bring into being a formidable coalition against Duke Charles. During the summer, Alsace, a possession of Austria but occupied by Burgundy, as security for a loan, revolted against the occupying power. The Emperor summoned Charles to evacuate, and on his refusal to comply called upon the Swiss to declare war. On one pretext or another, each member of the coalition withdrew, but the Swiss, fighting alone, completely crushed the Burgundian power. An inordinate love of money – they sold the rich province of the Franche-Comté to Austria – and jealousy of one another – it seemed Bern would alone profit from the conquests – prevented the Confederates reaping full advantage of their resounding victories.

During the Burgundian war Fribourg and Solothurn fought side by side with the Confederates. These two towns had for some time been allies of the Swiss, but now, after the successful conclusion of the war, they wanted to be admitted into the Confederation. The country districts felt that their admission would tip the balance at the diets in favour of the towns, and were, as a consequence, against it. Early in 1477 the original cantons with Glarus and Zug (now more identified with the country districts than with the towns) made an agreement with the Bishop of Constance; there was nothing inflammable in it, but it was a sign of the times that these five were together. Then during Lent came the plunder expedition already mentioned, which succeeded in stampeding the three towns, Zurich, Bern and Lucerne, first of all into making formal complaints and then into coming to an agreement, in May, with Fribourg and Solothurn. Since Lucerne's original alliance with the Ur cantons had precluded each member from making further alliances without the consent of the other members, this agreement of the five towns took the novel form of each town according to all the people of the other towns, the rights of citizenship (such an agreement is somewhat familiar today on account of Winston Churchill's offer to the French, in June 1940). It is hardly surprising the Ur cantons refused to consider this distinction, exonerated Lucerne from a breach of its alliance with them, but Lucerne stood its ground, affirming its unlimited right to grant citizenship to whomsoever it chose.

From the summer of 1477 until December 1481 there were then two conflicts: a general one concerning the admission of Fribourg and Solothurn into the Confederation, dividing the town and country cantons, and a more local one dividing Lucerne and the Ur cantons, particularly the neighbouring Unterwalden. Brother Klaus was active as peacemaker in both disputes. The extent of Lucerne's confidence in him – confidence which not even the Entlebuch rising shook – is revealed by the town account books. These 'petty cash books' contain several entries relating to the expenses of their envoys to Brother Klaus in the Ranft, and, even more interesting than this 'expenses account', an indication among the entries covering the weeks from the middle of July to the middle of August 1481 of '7 gulden paid to Peter Kundig, for a tunic for Brother Klaus'. During one of these last years of his life Brother Klaus assisted at the famous procession at Lucerne in honour of the Blessed Virgin Mary held on the eve of Lady Day. The special religious celebrations connected with the procession lasted three days, and the hermit stayed for them. As he made to return to the Ranft he was detained by a prominent member of the town council, a man belonging to the family Russ. This man earnestly begged him to leave behind his old tattered tunic and to accept a new one. The scene can be so easily imagined: at first, Brother Klaus modestly refused, but then, after much persuasion, agreed, and went off home in a new habit of grey cloth. If this is the tunic referred to in the account book, it looks uncommonly as though there was a 'conspiracy' among the town councillors, who had a tunic made by Peter Kundig and kept it ready for Brother Klaus's coming in March of 1482. An entry in the week 16-22

December 1481, i.e. before the definitive settlement at Stans, of forty gulden to Brother Klaus for a Mass in perpetuity in his chapel, shows Lucerne's gratitude. It proves too that they did not fear further complications and considered that his work of pacification was concluded.

While this more local dispute was running its course, the general one also seemed to be heading towards a settlement, thanks in part to the country cantons having given way on certain secondary points. It may well be that Brother Klaus was responsible for this softening of the country cantons' attitude. They remained adamant, however, that Fribourg and Solothurn were not to be admitted as equals into the Confederation, and that the towns were to abandon their 'citizenship-agreement'.

The Diet of Stans

A peaceful solution by way of compromise, perhaps elaborated and certainly encouraged by Brother Klaus, was by November 1481 on everyone's lips. The eight cantons were first to make a full alliance among themselves – the first scheme for this was drawn up in 1478 – and then the eight, on one part, would make an alliance with Fribourg and Solothurn, on the other part. In this way the Ur cantons would not have completely lost the position they clung to so tenaciously, and yet the new towns would have been fully allied to the Confederates. It was with this solution in view that, after having discussed and settled on their line of action, the cantons sent plenipotentiaries to a diet at Stans, on 18 December 1481. Petermann Etterlin, of Lucerne, a contemporary, considered even the convening of this diet was due to Klaus's efforts. It had probably cost the leaders of the original canton not a little to agree to this solution, and their anger knew no bounds when they heard that the delegates of Solothurn had only powers to agree to a full alliance of the ten districts, while the Fribourg envoys (already unwelcome to the farmers of the Ur cantons on account of their foreign tongue) had not been delegated any powers at all. The discussions led nowhere and in the evening of the 21st, St Thomas's Day, it seemed the outcome of it all would be a gruesome civil war.

During 1481, Heinrich am Grund, the intimate friend of Brother Klaus, had been named parish priest of Stans, a nomination which proved to be not without importance for the further existence of Switzerland. He seems to have been well informed of the state of affairs at the diet, and in the night of the 21st–22nd, realizing how close disaster was, he got up and went with all haste to Brother Klaus to tell him of the grave situation. Meanwhile all hope of agreement vanished, and the various delegates planned to leave in the afternoon, to go home and look to their own affairs for no one expected anything but war. Diebold Schilling, son of the Lucerne town clerk, who was present as his father's substitute, described how, just when all were making their preparations to depart, the parish priest, bathed in perspiration, arrived from Brother Klaus. He hurried from inn to inn begging the delegates for God's sake and for Brother Klaus's sake, to reassemble to hear the hermit's advice and opinion. Brother Klaus's prestige was such that the delegates did reassemble to hear his message, destined only for them; Diebold Schilling continues: '. . . bad as things had been in the morning, yet through his message they improved so much that within an hour everything was settled.' Schilling senior drew up the documents, and his son describes how a new charter was drawn up, and how the bells rang for joy that evening. The very first sentence of the proceedings of the diet of Stans, 22 December 1481, bears witness to 'the loyalty, the pains and the labour' which Brother Klaus had devoted to a peaceful settlement, and it expresses the gratitude of all.

Although Brother Klaus's message was destined only for the delegates, its import – at least in part – can be gathered from the result. His influence would seem to have persuaded the Solothurn delegates to go beyond the limits set them, and to accept the proposed union with the eight cantons; the Fribourg envoys, 'guaranteed' by Zurich, Bern and Lucerne, followed suit. If earlier Brother Klaus's influence had been exerted above all on the country cantons, now, at this final step, it was the delegates of the towns who followed his advice, so far as they were competent to do so. It was possible to settle everything so quickly because preliminary drafts had been made even before the diet. Brother Klaus's great work was the reconciling of conflicting wills, the bringing together of men who were on the point of war (a war which, in view of the European situation, would probably have meant the end of the Swiss Confederation), and of bringing them together in a constructive peaceful spirit so that they might formulate an act – the Covenant of Stans – which has been called the first Swiss constitutional law, an act which right up to the time of the French Revolution was to regulate the relations of the Confederates among themselves. If this time Solothurn and Fribourg are only accepted in a charter in which they form one party and the eight the other, they figure as equals in the pact made twenty years later when Basle and Schaffhausen entered the Confederation.

There are extant two letters, written in the days immediately following the diet at Stans; one of the letters is from Schwyz, a country district, and the other from Solothurn, one of the new towns. Each shows deep appreciation of Brother Klaus's part in bringing an end to 'the tension between town and country districts which had lasted so long', and tells of the joy that had taken hold of the assembly, and how in their joy they had had the church bells rung and a solemn Te Deum sung. Even more interesting, however, are the two letters written on 29 December by the assembled councillors of Solothurn to Brother Klaus and to the parish priest of Stans (things had been settled so quickly that they had forgotten to find out his name). Besides the letters, they sent to Brother Klaus twenty gulden for a Mass at the Ranft chapel in perpetuity, in token of their gratitude and veneration, and to Heinrich am Grund a copy of the legend of St Ursus, patron of Solothurn.

On that evening, when the bells rang out from the church at Sachseln down in the valley, surely Dorothea understood and appreciated something of what, under God, she and her husband had obtained for Switzerland by their separation in 1467.

Nicholas gives help

It would be wrong if, because of the foregoing pages, the impression were given that the majority of those who came to seek advice and help from Brother Klaus were connected with political affairs. From the very first year he was in the Ranft, individuals came to him with their personal problems and troubles. There is of course record of only comparatively few of these visitors, yet the various documents which provide a cross-section of the many who did come give some idea of the hermit's role as counsellor and guide, and at the same time give a vivid picture of the Ranft.

Only one contemporary document lets us glimpse Brother Klaus as 'spiritual director', that is, speaking and advising alone with someone who has come to him seeking light on a personal problem. This is a letter to a certain Walter, written by the 'young man from Burgdorf' as he has come to be called. Walter had asked his friend to tell him what he had heard from the lips of Brother Klaus, and the letter is the reply to that request.

> Eternal blessings in Our Lord! Beloved Walter, my brother . . . I will accede to your request, but I am ashamed that I asked such a man so little, yet on the other hand I am comforted in the knowledge that with others whose custom it is to ask many questions it delighted him to speak a lot. This I have learnt from others.
>
> When I went to him the first time I only put him one question, namely, whether it was permissible for me to settle in this neighbourhood to serve God, even though my parents knew nothing nor was I clear in my conscience about it. The man of God replied shortly: 'If you want to serve God you must not bother about anyone; but if you want to stay here in order to have a good time, you would do better to remain at home to look after your parents.' Satisfied with this answer I left him, in my foolishness not questioning him further about God or divine things . . .

Brother Klaus's pithy answer almost needs a commentary to be adequately appreciated: he is telling the young man that if he is really in earnest about serving God no consideration of his parents should stand in the way of his decision; further that he must not get a false idea of the eremitical life, and if he wants to have 'a good time' he would do better not to come. Having pointed this out he leaves it to the young man to make his own decision.

> 'However when I was back in Burgdorf,' the letter continues, 'I ever more frequently turned over in my mind what vocation to choose to serve God; I decided to apply to him once more.

99

But when I came to the hermitage to take counsel of the man of God, I did not find him. Only after I had waited for a long time did I meet the man I was longing for, and when I hurried towards him he stretched out his hand and said: "Welcome." Whereupon I replied: "You too are welcome to me; how long have I been praying for your arrival!" And then I went on: "I was here many days ago and asked whether I might stay in this district to serve God, unbeknown to my parents, and you gave me an answer which satisfied me. Now however, having decided to serve God in my own district, and free of my former scruple, I have come to ask your advice as to the state in which I should serve God." When he heard that, he sat himself down on a heap of stones and I sat at his feet, and he asked what state of life attracted me.

'Here I find it necessary to insert something I should have mentioned earlier. While I was having to wait for Brother Klaus's return home I went to Brother Ulrich, whom I feel sure is a special friend of God, and told him about myself and above all how much I was attracted to the eremitical life, and explained to him how long I had been troubled, and how I thought it well to stay for the moment, as I was, until I had collected money enough to build a hut and garden and to procure utensils needed to keep body and soul together. He replied that what I had proposed pleased him well and I left him with this decided. But what I have to say now is quite remarkable. When Brother Klaus asked me what state of life attracted me, all I had meant to say stuck in my throat, and I was unable to say a single word about all I had weighed in my mind for so long, and mentioned instead the vocation of a Carthusian or a Friar Minor. He replied that he thought a lot of the vocation of the Observants of Basle, "but I could not live in that order, because of the instability, that is to say they are sent from province to province," he said. I concluded that he preferred the Carthusians on account of their stability. I asked him whether it was not a pity that the Carthusians in community owned property. He replied: "in whatever order you are you have to live on alms. If the Carthusians have through alms accumulated so much property that it suffices for them, then they no longer need to send out their members to beg." This answer did away with my doubt.

'Then I asked: "in what way should one meditate on the Passion of Christ? Should one imagine to oneself Christ as though he were suffering now, and suffer with him as though it were one's brother suffering, or should one think of it as something past, bearing in mind that Christ has already overcome it all and reigns in glory, and so rejoice with him that he is so happy and that all his sufferings are at an end?" He replied: "It is good whichever way you do it," adding "for God knows how to arrange things so that praying can be as attractive as going dancing, or on the contrary it can be like fighting a war." When he mentioned dancing, small-minded that I was, I looked at him somewhat put out, as though I had been shocked that such a man should mention dancing. At once he saw how things were and repeated the word saying: "Yes, as though one were going dancing."

'Then further I complained to him how weak I was in persevering in my good intentions and how at the first opportunity I would turn again to what was forbidden, so that I was no longer in union with God as before. He replied that one should get quickly up again. While I was talking to him about myself, to my shame I must admit that I let fall something that sounded like boasting, whereupon, not slow in letting his inner zeal for righteousness be seen, he said: "You should not boast about the good that is in you."

'This little, out of much, I have noted down in so far as I could remember it, and have kept rather to the meaning than to the words.'

Once more Brother Klaus's delightful simplicity stands out in this scene with the somewhat scrupulous youngster, as he sits down on a heap of stones with the visitor seated at his feet to make him feel absolutely at his ease. It is certainly very interesting to see how much Brother Klaus appreciated the Carthusians, but there is no means of knowing whether the young man became one.

In the acts of the process in view of the beatification, there are other scenes with a rather more obviously miraculous flavour, which, although no longer coming from contemporaries, yet ring true and suggest an oral tradition among the local people. Some of them are worth describing.

The most influential of the Obwalden public figures of the second half of the fifteenth century, Hans Heintzli – nine times *Landamman* between 1450 and 1477 – went to visit Brother Klaus while an epidemic was raging in the district. He told the hermit that for safety's sake he had sent his two sons away to a place free of the plague, and asked what he thought of the arrangement. Brother Klaus answered Hans Heintzli he should take care he had not whisked his sons out of heaven into hell. In fact both sons met violent deaths in later years. One of them, Denis, became *Landamman* in 1485, but the following year was murdered in front of his house by a certain Walter Isner of Kerns, while the other was thrown from an unruly horse, and did not recover from his injuries. It is rather interesting to see that Hans Heintzli should have come to see Brother Klaus, for he accepted annuities from abroad and was in favour of foreign alliances, both of which policies Brother Klaus outspokenly opposed.

In Kerns a woman suspected her husband of adultery with their neighbour. On one occasion she had even been convinced she had seen the two of them in a field behind a thicket, and had fetched a knife intending to kill the woman, but when she had reached the spot there was no one there at all. Her suspicions had so worked on her imagination that she was 'seeing things'. Determined however to be quite sure she went to the neighbour's house, and there she found the woman with her baby at her breast. Thoroughly confused she determined to go to Brother Klaus in the Ranft to seek his advice. She found a great crowd in the chapel and in the cell. For a long time she waited while in their turn people went in to ask advice. Then she began to feel again that her suspicions were well founded, and she decided to go home since she would hardly get in to Brother Klaus that evening, as there were still so many people waiting. Just as she was making up her mind to go, Brother Klaus came out of the cell into the chapel, where there were still many people, both men and women, and said: 'There is a woman here wanting my advice; she can go home in peace, she is doing the pair of them an injustice, they are not guilty.' After he had said this, he turned round and went back into his cell. The people looked at one another not knowing to whom he had spoken, but the woman knew and was at once comforted and freed of her doubt; she thanked God and Brother Klaus for this, and then went happily home.

The following incident, which occurred about 1485 and concerned a farmer from Kerns, named Renngger, seems somewhat fantastic if we forget that 'in England, almost to within living memory, animals – cows, hens, sheep – were thought particularly susceptible to "ill-wishing" or "overlooking" by people with a grudge against their owners, and that carthorses still wear the elaborately patterned brasses whose original purpose was to repel those malign glances.' (Renée Haynes, *The Hidden Springs*, London, 1961, p.170.) Another passage from this book is worth citing: 'The widespread belief that witches could "ill-wish" cattle and fowls might be dismissed as the purest superstition but for the fact that cases of a reverse nature are still to be found, in which animals appear to respond well to the ministrations of "healers". I came across the traces of one myself in Aberystwyth in 1945 . . . He was apparently very successful and much respected; and by all accounts his treatment was conducted entirely by suggestion' (p.55). Suspecting a woman of being a witch Renngger had made up his mind to accuse her to the *Landamman*, but decided first of all to speak to Brother Klaus about the matter. His suspicions had been aroused because for three years, as he had passed her house on his way up to the alpine pastures, she had praised his herd and wished him luck, and then shortly afterwards the best of his animals had died. He thought this ill-luck was because she had cast a spell on the beasts. With his ten-year-old son he went to the Ranft. There Brother Klaus came towards him and told him he was unjust towards the woman, and he should go and ask her pardon for his suspicions, assuring him that his cattle would no longer come to any harm if he did so, since the devil had been given power to injure the animals because he had judged the woman so rashly. As the two men went on talking the little boy became restless and impatient to go home; Brother Klaus then clapped his hand on the lad's shoulder and said: 'You will live to a ripe enough age!' In fact he did not die until 1565, having reached his ninetieth year.

Some of those who wended their way to the Ranft came as part of the sentence they had been given for some crime, others came to fulfil a vow. On one occasion an adulterer came to question the hermit. But Brother Klaus took him out of his cell to the bank of the Melchaa, which is a roaring torrent at that spot, saying that he wanted to show him what happens after this life to those who live in sin. The man then saw two figures surrounded by flames leaping in and out of the water, and he felt ill at the sight of them. Then back in the chapel with Brother Klaus he let himself be corrected and consoled, and at home he put his life in order. There seem to have been visitors too who came to scoff, like the cattle-dealer from Constance, who had lost his fortune by careless management. He told various people that he had heard a lot about Brother Klaus, and that he intended to go and find out what he knew. So he went, with an enormous purse at his belt to give the impression that he was on his way to buy cattle. But Brother Klaus said to him: 'You come here as though you were a wealthy merchant, intending to make great purchases, but you haven't got a farthing in your purse.' Red with shame, the man beat a hasty retreat.

Dorothea and the children came to Brother Klaus for advice and help, and Peter continued to visit his brother. There is sadly all too little known about Dorothea during these years. Here and there she does come into the picture, as when Hans von Waldheim talked to her in the chapel or when Klaus got her to prepare a meal for the hungry Ulrich; it seems clear however that her relations with her hermit-husband were full of a deep understanding, and that he had no fear she would intrude on his solitude, however near they lived to one another. She had struggled not to let him go, and had given her consent only unwillingly, but their tremendous sacrifice, when at last fully consented to by both of them, can only have drawn them closer together. The oneness that can come from a separation, when it is fully accepted because of the conviction that it is what God wants, is part of the hundredfold promised by Christ. This has never been sufficiently stressed where Dorothea and Klaus are concerned. It undoubtedly sheds a warm light on what has too often been depicted in a rather coldly negative way, and it is a reminder that although God is a jealous God He is never outdone in generosity.

Other relatives also came to see the hermit, and there is one charming incident recorded of a young cousin, Verena Kiser, who often visited Brother Klaus with her mother-in-law. One day soon after her wedding she came, as usual, with her mother-in-law, to the Ranft. From the context it seems they had come to ask Brother Klaus to pray for the blessing of children for Verena. She was wearing a new dress, most probably the Obwalden costume still worn on great occasions by the women of the canton and the older woman who had made the dress did her best to get Brother Klaus to say what he thought of it. He looked at Verena and said: 'Were you in heaven wearing that dress for vanity's sake, you would have to leave, for God would not put up with it!' He insisted on the danger of vanity which creeps in so easily when women do their best to look nice, but he seems to have admired the dress all the same! He promised Verena she would have lots of children (she had eleven) and foretold an incident when she would lose her temper with them, and told her to think of him when it happened. This whole episode is related in the process to indicate that Brother Klaus had the gift of foreseeing the future.

There is another scene connected with clothes, which shows Teddy boys are not peculiar to our times. A young man came to Brother Klaus with clothes of an unusual cut, a fashion that had crept into the country at the time, and asked how he liked them. Brother Klaus replied that where the heart was good everything was in order, yet, he added, that he would wish the heart to be good in such a way that the young man would stop wearing such clothes. The two thoughts in this reply are not as contradictory, as at first sight, they appear; Klaus saw that it was possible to follow the fashion without doing wrong, but at the same time it was clear to him that fashion is not something quite indifferent, but is a mirroring of the moral standards of a people, and in this case perhaps even a cause of a lowering of accepted standards, all of which was probably quite unknown to the young man in newfangled clothes.

The country folk were not the only ones who came to the hermit for spiritual advice and help – even prominent churchmen came. Bishop Otto of Constance came to him not long after his election. The diocese was sadly divided at the time, as there had been an electoral struggle after the death of Bishop Hermann in 1474; the papal nominee, Ludwig of Freiberg, was supported by the Duke of Tyrol and the Count of Wurtemberg, while Otto, who had been elected by the chapter, was upheld by the Emperor and by the Confederates. For six years vain attempts were made to settle this affair, but the diocese was only united under one bishop, in 1480, when Ludwig died. After Bishop Otto had visited Brother Klaus he spoke most highly of his life and virtues, and said that he was pleased God had raised up such a hermit in his diocese. Thanks to Klaus he felt sure of greater success in all his undertakings. The bishop renewed the alliance with the Swiss which his predecessor had concluded five years before, and his efforts for reform were certainly seconded by the hermit in the Ranft.

It is worth mentioning that Brother Klaus was thought to have influence not only with the Confederates but even with the Duke of Austria. This appears in the Klingental convent affair. The wrongs and rights, the ins and outs, the different motives of the conflicting parties of this affair are so entangled that it is difficult to avoid falsifying the reality in attempting to give a brief resumé of the efforts to introduce and keep going a reform at the Dominican convent at Klingental, Basle. It must suffice to indicate that one party in the struggle – the party which at first glance appears to have justice entirely on its side, and, ultimately, to suffer quite unjustly – the Dominicans of Basle, not only sent Brother Ulrich, the provincial procurator, to see Brother Klaus to discuss the sorry business with him on the eve of the Epiphany, 1482, but also wrote, later that month, asking him to approach the Duke of Austria on their behalf as had been arranged, and promising to meet the expenses. If that letter did get written it has not survived. Perhaps it is a sign of his influence that Hans, his son, then *Landamman* of Obwalden, and representing both Obwalden and Nidwalden at the conference, which decided the dispute so disastrously for the Dominicans and for the cause of religion in general, did not affix his seal to the document of settlement.

Knowing something of the influence Brother Klaus had over the Confederates – perhaps also believing it to be much more than it was – the town of Constance in 1482, and the Duke of Milan in 1483, both approached the hermit to make use of his good offices.

The occupation of Thurgovia by the Confederates after the war of 1460 had led to differences between the victorious Swiss and the town of Constance; before the Austrians had been driven out, the town had had various rights, which it considered still held good, while the Confederates wanted to exercise absolute sovereignty. Eventually, on 26 January 1482, the *Burgermeister* and the Council of Constance, confident of the justice of their position and in the goodwill they had shown in seeking a peaceful solution, wrote to Brother Klaus informing him of the situation in the hope he could put their point of view in a favourable light, and, at the same time, asking him to pray for a just agreement. Their letter implies clearly they feared the occupying cantons, despite the good offices of Bern (acting as intermediary), might resort to warlike measures to get their way. Brother

Klaus's reply is worth giving in full; he does not promise more than he is able, and the letter seems to give a glimpse of how little he felt he could do apart from his prayer and love.

The name of Jesus be your greeting! I wish you great good, and desire that you should participate in every good action I do. I have understood your letter. Your request that I should pray for you to God I have also understood. I will do so faithfully, but in all things God's will be done. As far as in me lies, I shall do my best that my words lead to peace, and influence the well-meaning in your favour. It is my counsel that you act considerately in this matter, for one good action brings another; but if things cannot be settled amicably, then at least let an equitable settlement be the next best thing. In confirmation whereof I have had my own seal printed at the end of this letter. God be with you. Given on the Wednesday before the feast of St Blaise (January 30) anno Domini 82. Brother Klaus von Fluohe. To the devout, provident and wise Burgermeister and Councillors of the town of Constance, my dear Fathers.

On 19 February Constance replied to Brother Klaus expressing gratitude not only for his prayer and his kind letter but also for his activity for peace and a settlement which they had 'felt'. In fact the negotiations dragged on; Bern, irritated by the difficulties put in the way, gave up the role of intermediary; this role was then accepted by the Bishop of Constance, and, to Brother Klaus's joy, a settlement was at last reached in February 1483 without recourse to arms.

The Milanese approach to Brother Klaus in the following year was also to seek his help to calm the rather aggressive Swiss. The unwise provision in the agreement of Stans, which allowed the individual cantons to pursue their own foreign policy, was made use of already in 1482 and 1483 by the original cantons, together with Zug, when they formed a tiny, violently anti-Milanese front. The trouble concerned certain customs and revenue privileges granted to the Confederates which they wanted extended to 'the districts, named or unnamed, through which one passed on the direct road to Milan', but which the Milanese government alleged they had already abused. The other districts, especially Lucerne, sought to mediate in the dispute.

Late in 1482 an envoy, Gabriel Morosini, came to Lucerne; in the spring of 1483, the duke, Galeazzo Maria Sforza Visconti, sent an additional representative, Bernardino Imperiali. Imperiali's letters to the Duke of Milan gave a vivid picture of his efforts towards a peaceful settlement in the midst of war-hungry soldiers, recently discharged from French service. The Milanese had found an influential helper in Ludwig Seiler, councillor and merchant of Lucerne. In June the three of them went together to Unterwalden, and while Seiler sought out the two *Landammänner* (of Obwalden and Nidwalden), Imperiali and Morosini went to the Ranft to Brother Klaus.

Back in Lucerne, Imperiali wrote on 27 June to the duke:

> ... while Ludwig was away, Gabriel and I visited the hermit, who is considered a saint because he does not eat. The Confederation has great faith in him. I spent an evening and a morning with him, and spoke much about these affairs. I found him informed about everything, and he says the term 'unnamed' is an affront; he has not spoken with the delegates of Unterwalden since their return from the diet at Baden. I let him know the honourable and just conditions your Excellency had offered the Confederates, and also the efforts Lucerne had made to date to bring about the acceptance of the formula. The affair pained and troubled him very much, and

110

he prayed God might grant peace. Since I knew one of his sons was Landamman of Unterwalden, I begged him to lay the affair before him . . . He said he would send him a memorandum to be read at the next council meeting . . .

The hermit begged me to present you with his greetings and compliments . . . and assured me of his sincere love for you, and asked that you should overlook trifles in order to live in peace with the Confederates. I made him a present of a yard of green satin, which pleased him very much, for he intends to use it to mount certain of the Duke of Burgundy's relics which the Confederates have recently presented to him . . .

From Milan the duke answered Imperiali on 5 July 1483: 'With reference to the hermit, we are convinced that he really has the sympathy and love for us and our affairs which he expressed, and we are pleased you provided him with the present you mentioned, and would that you thank him on our behalf for his friendly greetings. Tell him we shall leave no stone unturned to live in peace with the Confederates in so far as that is compatible with our honour and the honour of our state.'

The difficulties were smoothed over and an agreement prepared so that Imperiali was able to return home in September; a month later the affair was definitively settled. The relics mentioned in Imperiali's letter were part of the fabulous booty taken by the Swiss from the Burgundians at Grandson. Charles the Bold's precious reliquary, which he had carried about with him, was taken, and although looters had made away with the valuable reliquary they had not dared to scatter the relics. These were distributed in March 1483 among the various districts, and some of them were given to Brother Klaus. The Milanese satin enabled him to house the relics once more in a decent manner.

Many of those who sought Brother Klaus's help made him, just as Imperiali had done, a present in money or in kind. It is surely worth recalling that among the donors was the Habsburg Archduke of Austria, 'the traditional enemy' of the Confederates. In 1473 he provided a chalice for use in the Ranft chapel, and, with his wife, Eleonora of Scotland, sent vestments and other objects, and later arranged for a Mass in perpetuity in the Ranft. For years now the presents and offerings had been accumulating and Brother Klaus in his turn could help those who came begging to him. In 1481 he contributed one gold gulden 'to God and St Oswald' for the building of the church of St Oswald at Zug. He also presented a chasuble to the chapel of St Joder at Altsellen, near Wolfenschiessen.

In 1482 there was sufficient in hand to set about endowing a benefice for the chapel in the Ranft. The official document, enacting all the necessary ordinances and suggestions, is preserved at Sachseln. The living is entrusted to the care of Obwalden councillors, who were to bestow it on a devout priest proposed by the parish of Sachseln. Should there later be a priest of his own family available Brother Klaus wished that he should be invited as chaplain, but this was only to be done if the priest were really worthy. Brother Klaus went into the details of the upkeep of the chapel and the duties of the chaplain; in case of need the chaplain was to supply in the parish, but it is stipulated that he would not be bound to this, if he did not care to leave the hermitage at all. One prescription is indicative of the hermit's care for parish unity: on Sundays and greater festivals the Mass in the Ranft was to be at an early hour so that those who had assisted at it would be able to reach Sachseln for the parish Mass. The first chaplain was Peter Bachtaler from Kerns. He was still in the Ranft when Brother Klaus died five years later. Probably he lived in the sacristan's house which was built that same year, and is still standing. A resident chaplain meant daily or frequent Mass and Brother Klaus must have been gratefully overjoyed.

While he was drawing up documents Brother Klaus thought of someone else. For thirteen years he had been faithfully and unobtrusively served as sacristan and general handyman by a certain Hensli (Johnnie). This otherwise unknown figure had never accepted any payment, but now Brother Klaus wanted him to be paid eight pounds a year out of the chaplain's benefice. If eight pounds proved not enough, whatever else he needed should be taken out of the offertory box. Brother Klaus's gratitude for this faithful devotion was quite clear; he expressed the hope that Hensli would not be dismissed, while Hensli for his part promised that should he save any money he would bequeath it to the chapel.

During 1482 the cantons showed further marks of gratitude to Brother Klaus. Once more it is an entry in an account book that tells what happened: in May, the Fribourg town council paid for a piece of white cloth and a piece of grey cloth for Brother Klaus and for Brother Ulrich (this inclusion of the hermit from the other side of the Melchaa is unusual); there was of course the tailor's bill to be paid, and the hire of a horse and the carrier's expenses to be met – all this was carefully noted. Towards the end of the year Bern sent Brother Klaus forty pounds for a Mass in perpetuity. The hermit's letter to the chief magistrate and the councillors of Bern is the only letter of thanks to the cantons that has been preserved. Its very uniqueness makes it doubly valuable. Suddenly, from a simple acknowledgment of their kindness towards him, the letter becomes a fervent appeal.

Owing to the absence of punctuation Brother Klaus's thought is, once or twice, not absolutely clear, but the letter is worth quoting close to the original.

> Your Worships. The Name of Jesus be your greeting! And we wish you much good and thank you for much good, and may the Holy Ghost be your final reward. I thank you earnestly and cordially for your friendly gift, recognizing indeed therein your fatherly love, which pleased me more than the gift. You must know that I am very satisfied, and had it been but the half I would still have been very satisfied. And if I could do anything to merit your love before God and the world, I would do it with a good will. The messenger, to whom you gave it, brought it to me very efficiently. I would like to recommend him to you, please.
>
> Out of love I am going to write more. Obedience is the greatest thing in heaven and on earth, and so you should take care to be obedient to one another; and wisdom is the most precious thing because it undertakes everything for the best. Peace is always in God, for God is peace and peace cannot be destroyed but discord has been destroyed. Take care then always to aim at preserving peace; protect widows and orphans as you have done up till now. If your good fortune on earth increases, be thankful to God for it, and then it will increase in heaven too. Public crimes should be put down, and justice should always be upheld. You should always bear the Passion of God in your hearts, for it is the greatest consolation for a man at his last end. Many are in doubt about the faith, and the devil brings about many a fall on account of the faith, and most of all on account of the faith. We must not nourish doubts about it, for as it has been established so it is; and I do not write to you because I think that you do not believe aright, I do not doubt that you are good Christians; I write thus to you by way of warning so that should the evil spirit tempt anyone he should resist all the

more chivalrously. No more. God be with you. Dated on St. Barbara's Day in the year 82. I have had my own seal printed on this letter. I, Brother Klaus von Flüe.

It is probably unnecessary to see anything prophetic in the hermit's warning to the Bernese to hold fast to the faith 'established', but Bern's passing over to the doctrines of the Reformation forty years later shows that the warning was needed. This letter is a good example of the kind of advice Brother Klaus gave on general political principles. Wölflin, mentioning that Brother Klaus was often consulted in important questions concerning the Confederation, said that all his counsels were in view of promoting the peace of the whole country, neighbourly unity, and the honour of God and obedience to his commandments. Gundelfingen mentions the advice given by the hermit that politicians should not allow themselves to be corrupted by gifts from foreign powers, that they should be guided by principles of justice rather than profit, and that they should not easily accept foreigners for naturalization lest they get involved in dishonest policies and even quite easily in wars with their neighbours.

Little attention was paid to this advice during the years after his death. Wölflin dedicated the 'Life' to Cardinal Schinner, but the ambitious prelate was honest enough to see the incongruity of pushing for the canonization of a man whose reiterated advice he was spurning so completely. The defeat at Marignano in 1515 brought the Swiss to their senses, but Zwingli more than once reminded his Catholic adversaries how little they paid heed to Klaus's advice.

There was no doubt about it; even after the agreement at Stans there was need of preaching peace and unity, and not least to the cantons nearest the Ranft. The country cantons were doing their utmost to withhold from the new towns the treatment as equals they had expected. It is most likely that it was in connection with this matter that towards the end of January 1482, Henmann Zeiss, the official town messenger of Solothurn, wended his way to Brother Klaus. In the following year the country cantons moved that the right of vote should be taken away from the new towns. All this throws further light on the tremendous influence Brother Klaus must have exerted in 1481 to bring the country cantons to a compromise.

If in the Klingental affair Brother Klaus does seem to have been able to influence his son, Hans, it looks as though this was something of an exception, and the impression remains that the hermit was rather like a prophet without honour in his own canton. A warlike spirit was abroad in the Ur cantons and most of all in Unterwalden; after the trouble with Milan had been settled, Unterwalden stirred up strife with the Emperor. Hans von Flüe was active in this wretched business, and he seems to have been in the pay of Rudolf and Jakob Motteli, and to have been responsible for the temper of the Obwalden rank and file.

It would be pleasant to have more news of the other children to set against this of Hans, for Klaus had not lost interest in them when he left home. Of one only, however, can something other than probable conjecture be recorded. Nicholas, the youngest child, who had been sixteen weeks old when his father left home, was in Paris at the university at this time. When one of his fellow students mentioned that he was going to Switzerland, he asked him to take two letters to his father. The student, who later was to tell the story of these letters to Wölflin, set off on the long journey to the Ranft, but before he got to Switzerland he lost one of the letters. Quite understandably he was not a little put out, and,

116

fearing his friend's father would be annoyed, it was only with some trepidation that he plucked up courage and decided to go on, with the remaining letter, to the Ranft. As he was approaching the chapel, Brother Klaus came down the slope, holding out towards him the letter that had been lost. He greeted the student in a friendly fashion, telling him that he knew it was he who had been entrusted by young Nicholas with the letter that had been lost, and assuring him there was nothing to worry about since it was found. Once again Wölflin's brevity is tantalizing, for surely the erstwhile student told him more about the meeting with his friend's father!

The Bear's Claw

During the first months of 1487, Brother Klaus must have thought of a vision he had had while he was still at home. This vision has already been alluded to. While Klaus was working at home one day, three men, whose dress and bearing indicated their nobility, came towards him. The first of them asked him: 'Klaus, will you give yourself body and soul into our hands?' He at once replied: 'I give myself to no one but to Almighty God; Him I desire to serve with all my strength.' At this reply they turned to each other and smiled happily. Turning again to him, the first of the three said: 'Since you have given yourself only to serve God Almighty, I promise you that the merciful God will deliver you from all your trials and troubles when you reach your seventieth year. Till then persevere patiently and I shall give you in eternal life the bear's claw and the banner of the victorious army; but I leave you now the cross; that cross is to remind you always of us.' At that they left him. Evidently the bear's claw, like the banner, is meant as a sign of his victory. When a bear-hunt had ended successfully a claw was cut off and hung as a trophy at the door of the hunter's house. The combat with the bear is symbolic of the combat with the devil, and most certainly Brother Klaus understood the symbolism and realized that carrying the cross was at once the condition of his victory and the means of obtaining it. That cross, by the grace of God, he had carried valiantly, and he must have longed ever more fervently for the promise as the days passed in 1487, for, Wölflin tells, he knew the day of his death.

Despite his complete detachment from all earthly things Brother Klaus was not spared a week of great physical suffering. He was seized by a most painful illness, which caused him acute pains in his bones and joints. Utterly emaciated by his long fast he was unable to find a position in which to obtain relief from his sufferings. After a week of pitiable agony, borne with great patience, he asked to receive the holy viaticum of the Body and Blood of Jesus Christ. Dorothea was probably fetched, and besides her we can presume that at least Hensli, and the friend to whom Brother Klaus had confided the date of his death and who had come to the Ranft to be near him, were present in the tiny cell. Brother Klaus received the Blessed Sacrament very reverently, and then, stretched out on the bare floor, thanking God, he died, in great agony. It was 21 March 1487, and Brother Klaus was seventy years old.

The news of his death spread quickly throughout the Confederation and to the neighbouring countries. In Lucerne the bells of St Peter's were tolled for him, and throughout the Confederation memorial services were held, while even across the frontier Sigmund, the Habsburg ruler of Austria, assisted at a solemn requiem for him

According to his own instructions the body was carried for

burial to the parish church at Sachseln. There, in the churchyard, a week later, on 28 March, the Wednesday of the fourth week in Lent, Brother Klaus was buried, in the presence of his wife and children and friends, and also of a large gathering of priests and lay-folk from the whole of Unterwalden, of two town councillors from Lucerne, and assuredly of representatives of the cantons. Next day Dorothea came to his grave to pray for him. When she was there a man approached her and told her he had seen the deceased Klaus in glorious radiance on the hillside, carrying in his hand a banner with on it a bear's claw, for all the powers of darkness had been overcome by his constancy.

Epilogue

On 13 April 1487 the Milanese envoys, blaming pressure of work for their tardiness in writing, sent from Zurich to inform the Duke of Milan of the Unterwalden hermit's death on the 21st of the preceding month. They added that as far as they knew he had not yet worked any further miracles, but that everyone was expecting him to do so. 'Everyone's' expectations did not go unfulfilled. The Sachseln parish register contains the description of twenty-three miraculous cures attributed to Brother Klaus's intercession during the first year after his death. Most of the people who came seeking to be cured were, naturally enough, from within the borders of the Confederation, but, already during this first year, there were pilgrims from abroad and among those cured of their illnesses were a convert Jew from Nuremberg and a fisherman from Denmark. It is not surprising that St Brother Klaus was soon known as the 'Doctor of the Swiss'. The cures have continued ever since; very many have been carefully recorded, and the more recent ones recorded with clinical precision, not least the two accepted in the canonization process, are most striking.

It would be a mistake to linger on the miracles, lest the impression be given that Brother Klaus's importance for our own time is simply one of intercession. The leaving of his wife and family, the long complete fast, the self-inflicted penances – all these are things which suggest the application to St Nicholas of the much used and misused tag: 'He is more to be admired than to be imitated.' To leave it at that would be to neglect, with considerable impoverishment, a figure whose importance was not uniquely for his own time and country and whose canonization was surely not reserved for the twentieth century without some providential reason. St Nicholas is an example to the world today just as he was to the Swiss in the fifteenth century.

Even if little value can be put on the authenticity of the collections of sayings and meditations popularly ascribed to St Nicholas he himself stands out as a living doctrine. If, as Jakob Burckhardt thought, the Swiss Confederation was the only country in Europe in which true liberty was combined with political responsibility in the existence of every citizen, Brother Klaus stands out as exemplifying this to a rare degree. In civic and political affairs he is sincere and honest, not hesitating to speak his mind when it seems right to do so even if it means making enemies, not hesitating even to withdraw completely when there is no other way of protesting effectively. Throughout his adult life, as a conscript no less than as a councillor and as a hermit, his 'statecraft' consisted above all in the spreading of peace. It is true to say that he was the first Swiss patriot, the first Swiss who constantly looked beyond the narrow interests of his own canton to the interests of the whole Confederation. He stands out as a symbol of unity among nations; in our own time, when it has been said with no little justice, that 'emotionally we are still at the stage of village patriotism for which everything outside our own front door is foreign and half-hostile,' St Nicholas is there to teach us where our true interests lie, and to make quite clear the distinction between patriotism and narrow-minded nationalism, for those who are already wary of themselves when they see hatred becoming equated to patriotism.

Even among disunited Christians Brother Klaus is today a

bond of union, for he is venerated in his own country by Catholics and Protestants alike; one of the most penetrating studies of his inner life is by a Protestant, Professor Dr Fritz Blanke. Not only among Christians of the West should he prove a bond of union. Dr Walter Nigg has characterized him as 'The Swiss Staretz', a profoundly apt title, which should help to endear him to the Orthodox in general, and to the Russians in particular. Dare one go even further and hope he will find admirers in India, for his life does present some resemblance to that of the Brahmin?

In his inner history St Nicholas has much to say to a generation enamoured of sincerity and conscious of the immensity of the tasks facing it. He learnt from a very early age to 'be still', and from that he learnt life and wisdom. He makes it abundantly clear that contemplation and prayer must precede action. He shows us not only the austere element in the life of faith, the tremendous ruthless passion that love of God is, but also that only in such intense love and faith do we live fully. Perhaps supreme in shaping and expressing genuine personality is a readiness unreservedly to serve God; that it was present in St Nicholas to a high degree does not need to be emphasized. His visions show too that he was not blind to the created reflections of God's beauty – mountains, music, palaces, all find their way into them – and here again he speaks to an age seeking after integrated personalities. The years of 'grievous trial' when he found no rest in anything, when even the presence of those dear to him in the circle of his family was irksome, moulded him and left a deep impress on him. Small wonder he was said, as Abbot Trithemius wrote, to have a quite remarkable gift for encouraging those who were sad and depressed. If the interpretation given of his 'flight from the Ranft' is correct then he must have learnt to think of himself as a failure, and the memory of what was well-nigh defeat must have given him both the quality of knowing himself as he really was, and the deep endless human sympathy that accompanies that knowledge when it is borne up by the realization of God's love. The hermit's warm friendliness, his affection and thoughtfulness to all and sundry were not superficial; even his courtesy was motivated by real love, and that is a power creative of unity among individuals and peoples.

Even the 'terrible vision' is important for us; because of that importance the iconography of Brother Klaus must not be made into something sickly and soft. It must be able to arouse in us the awareness of God as a reality. Klaus was, at the moment of that vision, a victim of Glory, and the 'true' statue or painting must let us glimpse the imprint of that Glory, so that we long to see face to face not only the saint but far more the Lord who aroused the wholehearted devotion of such a rich personality.

One final point, a unique trait, must be mentioned. After St Nicholas left home he became known to all as 'Brother'. Today still he is affectionately called 'Brother Klaus'. He left all human ties to cling to God alone, and then he found them all again a hundredfold. For everyone he was a brother, and he was deeply conscious of all that glorious title implied. There is nothing we need so much today as the sense of our brotherhood with all men – no matter what their race or colour – but that is fundamentally dependent on our acceptance of the fatherhood of God. Here too St Brother Klaus can help us, and as we repeat his glorious prayer he will surely teach us, his brothers and sisters, the great programme it sets before us and asks of God:

> My Lord and my God, take me from myself
> and give me to thyself as wholly thine.

Appendix

The pre-natal Visions and the precocious Memory

From early times the following verses of St Luke's Gospel have been interpreted as indicating the privilege of a premature use of reason for St John the Baptist. 'When Elizabeth heard Mary's greeting the baby stirred in her womb . . . Elizabeth said "Who am I, that the mother of my Lord should visit me? I tell you, when your greeting sounded in my ears, the baby in my womb leapt for joy." ' (ch. I, vv. 41 & 44)

Theologians in the past were of the opinion that this privilege of a premature use of reason was reserved uniquely to Christ and to His precursor, but research undertaken during the last twenty to thirty years has thrown much light on the hidden life of the unborn child. It is generally recognized now that the unborn child is an aware reacting human being, who from the sixth month (and maybe before) leads an active feeling life. They experience primitive emotions and these primitive emotions begin the shaping of their attitudes and expectations about themselves in later life. The months in the womb are a crucial time in a person's development, not just physically but emotionally.

It is fascinating to recall that there is a charming Jewish tradition of a conversation between God and embryos in their mothers' womb (*The Midrash on Psalms* vol. I, p. 125, Gale University Press, 1959) while M-L. von Franz (in her book on Nicholas, p. (18)) mentions instances from fairy tales and from mythology of children speaking while in their mother's womb.

Dr F. Elkisch, a disciple of C.J. Jung, who himself was keenly interested in Nicholas, pointed out the existence of unique and rare phenomena which exist as subjective realities but which cannot be verified by any objective causal way of approach. The mental structure of the person to whom these phenomena occur functions on a different level to that of most people, but that does not suffice for their reality to be denied. These pre-natal visions and this precocious memory would seem to be such rare phenomena.

Bibliography

Sources:

Robert Durrer, *Bruder Klaus. Die ältesten Quellen über den seligen Niklaus von Flüe, sein Leben und seinen Einfluss*, 2 vols, Sarnen, 1917-1921. In addition to the above-mentioned biographies Durrer printed in these volumes the Sachseln Parish Register, the relevant passages of Hans von Waldheim's diary, various passages of Eichorn and all the other known roughly contemporary writings about St Nicholas, prefacing each with an introduction and providing useful notes.

Heinrich Gundelfingen, Canon of Beromunster, *Historia Nicolai Underwaldensis eremitae*, 1488 (printed in R. Durrer, *Bruder Klaus. Die altesten Quellen . . .* , Sarnen, 1917-1921, pp. 423-45).

Otto Karrer, *Eine unbekannte Nachricht über Niklaus von der Flüe*, in Schweizerische Rundschau, 1927-8, pp. 258-62.

Alan Neame, *The Holy Maid of Kent. 1506-1534*, Hodder and Stoughton, London, 1971.

P. Adelbert Wagner, O.M. Cap., *Der Geschichtsfreund*, 1928, vol.83, pp. 104-16, published the text of a ms. found at Lucerne containing the three visions written down by Casper am Buel.

Heinrich Wölflin, the first official biography, published probably in 1501 (printed in R. Durrer, op. cit. pp. 524-55).

Jeanne d'Arc, edited by T. Douglas Murray, William Heinemann, London, 1902.

Biographies and Studies:

A. Andrey, *Le Saint Vivant*, Geneva, 1939.

Fritz Blanke, *Bruder Klaus von Flüe. Seine innere Geschichte*, Zurich, 1948.

Heinrich Federer, *Nikolaus von Flüe*, Frauenfeld, 1929. This was a series of articles published as a book posthumously.

Mgr. Charles Journet, *Saint Nicolas de Flüe*, Neuchatel, 1947.

G.R. Lamb, *Brother Nicholas. A Life of St. Nicholas of Flüe*, London, 1955.

Benoit Lavaud, O.P., *Vie profonde de Nicolas de Flüe*, Friborg, 1942, and *Nicolas de Flüe et les Peres du Desert*, Friborg, 1942.

Marie McSwigan, *Athlete of Christ. St. Nicholas of Flüe 1417-1487*, Westminster Md., 1959.

Walter Nigg, 'The Swiss Staretz. Nicholas von Flüe', in *Great Saints*, London, 1948, pp. 91-116.

Konstantin Vokinger, *Bruder Klaus. Sein Leben*, Stans, 1947.

M-L von Franz, *Die Visionen des Niklaus von Flüe*, Studien aus dem C.G. Jung Institut Zurich IX, Zurich, 1959.

Leonard von Matt, *Der heilige Bruder Klaus. Offizielles Gedenkbuch der Heiligsprechung*, Zurich, 1947.

Christina Yates, *Brother Klaus. Man of Two Worlds*, York, 1989.